# State of the Union Addresses

## ULYSSES GRANT

Published in 1869

# TABLE OF CONTENTS

# STATE OF THE UNION ADDRESSES

# STATE OF THE UNION ADDRESSES

December 6, 1869
To the Senate and House of Representatives:

In coming before you for the first time as Chief Magistrate of this great nation, it is with gratitude to the Giver of All Good for the many benefits we enjoy. We are blessed with peace at home, and are without entangling alliances abroad to forebode trouble; with a territory unsurpassed in fertility, of an area equal to the abundant support of 500,000,000 people, and abounding in every variety of useful mineral in quantity sufficient to supply the world for generations; with exuberant crops; with a variety of climate adapted to the production of every species of earth's riches and suited to the habits, tastes, and requirements of every living thing; with a population of 40,000,000 free people, all speaking one language; with facilities for every mortal to acquire an education; with institutions closing to none the avenues to fame or any blessing of fortune that may be coveted; with freedom of the pulpit, the press, and the school; with a revenue flowing into the National Treasury beyond the requirements of the Government. Happily, harmony is being rapidly restored within our own borders. Manufactures hitherto unknown in our country are springing up in all sections, producing a degree of national independence unequaled by that of any other power.

These blessings and countless others are intrusted to your care and mine for safe-keeping for the brief period of our tenure of office. In a short time we must, each of us, return to the ranks of the people, who have conferred upon us our honors, and account to them for our stewardship. I earnestly desire that neither you nor I may be condemned by a free and enlightened constituency nor by our own consciences.

Emerging from a rebellion of gigantic magnitude, aided, as it was, by the sympathies and assistance of nations with which we were at peace, eleven States of the Union were, four years ago, left without legal State governments. A national debt had been contracted; American commerce was almost driven from the seas; the industry of one-half of the country had been taken from the control of the capitalist and placed where all labor rightfully belongs—in the keeping of the laborer. The work of restoring State governments loyal to the Union, of protecting and fostering free labor, and providing means for paying the interest on the public debt has received ample attention from Congress. Although your efforts have not met with the success in all particulars that might have been desired, yet on the whole they have been more successful than could have been reasonably anticipated.

Seven States which passed ordinances of secession have been fully restored to their places in the Union. The eighth (Georgia) held an election at which she ratified her constitution, republican in form, elected a governor, Members of Congress, a State legislature, and all other officers required. The governor was duly installed, and the legislature met and performed all the acts then required of them by the reconstruction acts of Congress. Subsequently, however, in violation of the constitution which they had just ratified (as since decided by the supreme court of the State), they unseated the colored members of the legislature and admitted to seats some members who are disqualified by the third clause of the fourteenth amendment to the Constitution—an article which they themselves had contributed to ratify. Under these circumstances I would submit to you whether it would not be wise, without delay, to enact a law authorizing the governor of Georgia to convene the members originally elected to the legislature, requiring each member to take the oath prescribed by the reconstruction acts, and none to be admitted who are ineligible under the third clause of the fourteenth amendment.

The freedmen, under the protection which they have received, are making rapid progress in learning, and no complaints are heard of lack of industry on their part where they receive fair remuneration for their labor. The means provided for paying the interest on the public debt, with all other expenses of Government, are more than ample. The loss of our commerce is the only result of the late rebellion which has not received sufficient attention from you. To this subject I call your earnest attention. I will not now suggest plans by which this object may be effected, but will, if necessary, make it the subject of a special message during the session of Congress.

At the March term Congress by joint resolution authorized the Executive to order elections in the States of Virginia, Mississippi, and Texas, to submit to them the constitutions which each had previously, in convention, framed, and submit the constitutions, either entire or in separate parts, to be voted upon, at the discretion of the Executive. Under this authority elections were called. In Virginia the election took place on the 6th of July, 1869. The governor and lieutenant-governor elected have been installed. The legislature met and did all required by this resolution and by all the reconstruction acts of Congress, and abstained from all doubtful authority. I recommend that her Senators and Representatives be promptly admitted to their seats, and that the State be fully restored to its place in the family of States. Elections were called in Mississippi and Texas, to commence on the 30th of November, 1869, and to last two days in Mississippi and four days in Texas. The elections have taken place, but the result is not known. It is to be hoped that the acts of the legislatures of these States, when they meet, will be such as to receive your approval, and thus close the work of reconstruction.

Among the evils growing out of the rebellion, and not yet referred to, is that of an irredeemable currency. It is an evil which I hope will receive your most earnest attention. It is a duty, and one of the highest duties, of Government to secure to the citizen a medium of exchange of fixed, unvarying value. This implies a return to a specie basis, and no substitute for it can be devised. It should be commenced now and reached at the earliest practicable moment consistent with a fair regard to the interests of the debtor class. Immediate resumption, if practicable, would not be desirable. It would compel the debtor class to pay, beyond their contracts, the premium on gold at the date of their purchase and would bring bankruptcy and ruin to thousands. Fluctuation, however, in the paper value of the measure of all values (gold) is detrimental to the interests of trade. It makes the man of business an involuntary gambler, for in all sales where future payment is to be made both parties speculate as to what will be the value of the currency to be paid and received. I earnestly recommend to you, then, such legislation as will insure a gradual return to specie payments and put an immediate stop to fluctuations in the value of currency.

The methods to secure the former of these results are as numerous as are the speculators on political economy. To secure the latter I see but one way, and that is to authorize the Treasury to redeem its own paper, at a fixed price, whenever presented, and to withhold from circulation all currency so redeemed until sold again for gold.

The vast resources of the nation, both developed and undeveloped, ought to make our credit the best on earth. With a less burden of taxation than the citizen has endured for six years past, the entire public debt could be paid in ten years. But it is not desirable that the people should be taxed to pay it in that time. Year by year the ability to pay increases in a rapid ratio.

7

But the burden of interest ought to be reduced as rapidly as can be done without the violation of contract. The public debt is represented in great part by bonds having from five to twenty and from ten to forty years to run, bearing interest at the rate of 6 per cent and 5 per cent, respectively. It is optional with the Government to pay these bonds at any period after the expiration of the least time mentioned upon their face. The time has already expired when a great part of them may be taken up, and is rapidly approaching when all may be. It is believed that all which are now due may be replaced by bonds bearing a rate of interest not exceeding 4 1/2 per cent, and as rapidly as the remainder become due that they may be replaced in the same way. To accomplish this it may be necessary to authorize the interest to be paid at either of three or four of the money centers of Europe, or by any assistant treasurer of the United States, at the option of the holder of the bond. I suggest this subject for the consideration of Congress, and also, simultaneously with this, the propriety of redeeming our currency, as before suggested, at its market value at the time the law goes into effect, increasing the rate at which currency shall be bought and sold from day to day or week to week, at the same rate of interest as Government pays upon its bonds.

The subjects of tariff and internal taxation will necessarily receive your attention. The revenues of the country are greater than the requirements, and may with safety be reduced. But as the funding of the debt in a 4 or a 4 1/2 per cent loan would reduce annual current expenses largely, thus, after funding, justifying a greater reduction of taxation than would be now expedient, I suggest postponement of this question until the next meeting of Congress.

It may be advisable to modify taxation and tariff in instances where unjust or burdensome discriminations are made by the present laws, but a general revision of the laws regulating this subject I recommend the postponement of for the present. I also suggest the renewal of the tax on incomes, but at a reduced rate, say of 3 per cent, and this tax to expire in three years.

With the funding of the national debt, as here suggested, I feel safe in saying that taxes and the revenue from imports may be reduced safely from sixty to eighty millions per annum at once, and may be still further reduced from year to year, as the resources of the country are developed.

The report of the Secretary of the Treasury shows the receipts of the Government for the fiscal year ending June 30, 1869, to be $370,943,747, and the expenditures, including interest, bounties, etc., to be $321,490,597. The estimates for the ensuing year are more favorable to the Government, and will no doubt show a much larger decrease of the public debt.

The receipts in the Treasury beyond expenditures have exceeded the amount necessary to place to the credit of the sinking fund, as provided by law. To lock up the surplus in the Treasury and withhold it from circulation would lead to such a contraction of the currency as to cripple trade and seriously affect the prosperity of the country. Under these circumstances the Secretary of the Treasury and myself heartily concurred in the propriety of using all the surplus currency in the Treasury in the purchase of Government bonds, thus reducing the interest-bearing indebtedness of the country, and of submitting to Congress the question of the disposition to be made of the bonds so purchased. The bonds now held by the Treasury amount to about seventy-five millions, including those belonging to the sinking fund. I recommend that the whole be placed to the credit of the sinking fund.

Your attention is respectfully invited to the recommendations of the Secretary of the Treasury for the creation of the office of commissioner of customs revenue; for the increase of salaries to certain classes of officials; the substitution of increased national-bank circulation to replace the outstanding 3 per cent certificates; and most especially to his recommendation for the repeal of laws allowing shares of fines, penalties, forfeitures, etc., to officers of the Government or to informers.

The office of Commissioner of Internal Revenue is one of the most arduous and responsible under the Government. It falls but little, if any, short of a Cabinet position in its importance and responsibilities. I would ask for it, therefore, such legislation as in your judgment will place the office upon a footing of dignity commensurate with its importance and with the character and qualifications of the class of men required to fill it properly.

As the United States is the freest of all nations, so, too, its people sympathize with all people struggling for liberty and self-government; but while so sympathizing it is due to our honor that we should abstain from enforcing our views upon unwilling nations and from taking an interested part, without invitation, in the quarrels between different nations or between governments and their subjects. Our course should always be in conformity with strict justice and law, international and local. Such has been the policy of the Administration in dealing with these questions. For more than a year a valuable province of Spain, and a near neighbor of ours, in whom all our people can not but feel a deep interest, has been struggling for independence and freedom. The people and Government of the United States entertain the same warm feelings and sympathies for the people of Cuba in their pending struggle that they manifested throughout the previous struggles between Spain and her former colonies in behalf of the latter. But the contest has at no time assumed the conditions which amount to a war in the sense of international law, or which would show the existence of a de facto political organization of the insurgents sufficient to justify a recognition of belligerency.

The principle is maintained, however, that this nation is its own judge when to accord the rights of belligerency, either to a people struggling to free themselves from a government they believe to be oppressive or to independent nations at war with each other.

The United States have no disposition to interfere with the existing relations of Spain to her colonial possessions on this continent. They believe that in due time Spain and other European powers will find their interest in terminating those relations and establishing their present dependencies as independent powers—members of the family of nations. These dependencies are no longer regarded as subject to transfer from one European power to another. When the present relation of colonies ceases, they are to become independent powers, exercising the right of choice and of self-control in the determination of their future condition and relations with other powers.

The United States, in order to put a stop to bloodshed in Cuba, and in the interest of a neighboring people, proposed their good offices to bring the existing contest to a termination. The offer, not being accepted by Spain on a basis which we believed could be received by Cuba, was withdrawn. It is hoped that the good offices of the United States may yet prove advantageous for the settlement of this unhappy strife. Meanwhile a number of illegal expeditions against Cuba have been broken up. It has been the endeavor of the Administration to execute the neutrality laws in good faith, no matter how unpleasant the task, made so by the sufferings we have endured from lack of like good faith toward us by other nations.

On the 26th of March last the United States schooner Lizzie Major was arrested on the high seas by a Spanish frigate, and two passengers taken from it and carried as prisoners to Cuba. Representations of these facts were made to the Spanish Government as soon as official information of them reached Washington. The two passengers were set at liberty, and the Spanish Government assured the United States that the captain of the frigate in making the capture had acted without law, that he had been reprimanded for the irregularity of his conduct, and that the Spanish authorities in Cuba would not sanction any act that could violate the rights or treat with disrespect the sovereignty of this nation.

The question of the seizure of the brig Mary Lowell at one of the Bahama Islands by Spanish authorities is now the subject of correspondence between this Government and those of Spain and Great Britain.

The Captain-General of Cuba about May last issued a proclamation authorizing search to be made of vessels on the high seas. Immediate remonstrance was made against this, whereupon the Captain-General issued a new proclamation limiting the right of search to vessels of the United States so far as authorized under the treaty of 1795. This proclamation, however, was immediately withdrawn.

I have always felt that the most intimate relations should be cultivated between the Republic of the United States and all independent nations on this continent. It may be well worth considering whether new treaties between us and them may not be profitably entered into, to secure more intimate relations—friendly, commercial, and otherwise.

The subject of an interoceanic canal to connect the Atlantic and Pacific oceans through the Isthmus of Darien is one in which commerce is greatly interested. Instructions have been given to our minister to the Republic of the United States of Colombia to endeavor to obtain authority for a survey by this Government, in order to determine the practicability of such an undertaking, and a charter for the right of way to build, by private enterprise, such a work, if the survey proves it to be practicable.

In order to comply with the agreement of the United States as to a mixed commission at Lima for the adjustment of claims, it became necessary to send a commissioner and secretary to Lima in August last. No appropriation having been made by Congress for this purpose, it is now asked that one be made covering the past and future expenses of the commission.

The good offices of the United States to bring about a peace between Spain and the South American Republics with which she is at war having been accepted by Spain, Peru, and Chile, a congress has been invited to be held in Washington during the present winter.

A grant has been given to Europeans of an exclusive right of transit over the territory of Nicaragua, to which Costa Rico has given its assent, which, it is alleged, conflicts with vested rights of citizens of the United States. The Department of State has now this subject under consideration.

The minister of Peru having made representations that there was a state of war between Peru and Spain, and that Spain was constructing, in and near New York, thirty gunboats, which might be used by Spain in such a way as to relieve the naval force at Cuba, so as to operate against Peru, orders were given to prevent their departure. No further steps having been taken by the representative of the Peruvian Government to prevent the departure of these vessels, and I not feeling authorized to detain the property of a nation with which we are at peace on a mere Executive order, the matter has been referred to the courts to decide.

The conduct of the war between the allies and the Republic of Paraguay has made the intercourse with that country so difficult that it has been deemed advisable to withdraw our representative from there.

Toward the close of the last Administration a convention was signed at London for the settlement of all outstanding claims between Great Britain and the United States, which failed to receive the advice and consent of the Senate to its ratification. The time and the circumstances attending the negotiation of that treaty were unfavorable to its acceptance by the people of the United States, and its provisions were wholly inadequate for the settlement of the grave wrongs that had been sustained by this Government, as well as by its citizens. The injuries resulting to the United States by reason of the course adopted by Great Britain during our late civil war—in the increased rates of insurance; in the diminution of exports and imports, and other obstructions to domestic industry and production; in its effect upon the foreign commerce of the country; in the decrease and transfer to Great Britain of our commercial marine; in the prolongation of the war and the increased cost (both in treasure and in lives) of its suppression could not be adjusted and satisfied as ordinary commercial claims, which continually arise between commercial nations; and yet the convention treated them simply as such ordinary claims, from which they differ more widely in the gravity of their character than in the magnitude of their amount, great even as is that difference. Not a word was found in the treaty, and not an inference could be drawn from it, to remove the sense of the unfriendliness of the course of Great Britain in our struggle for existence, which had so deeply and universally impressed itself upon the people of this country.

Believing that a convention thus misconceived in its scope and inadequate in its provisions would not have produced the hearty, cordial settlement of pending questions, which alone is consistent with the relations which I desire to have firmly established between the United States and Great Britain, I regarded the action of the Senate in rejecting the treaty to have been wisely taken in the interest of peace and as a necessary step in the direction of a perfect and cordial friendship between the two countries. A sensitive people, conscious of their power, are more at ease under a great wrong wholly unatoned than under the restraint of a settlement which satisfies neither their ideas of justice nor their grave sense of the grievance they have sustained. The rejection of the treaty was followed by a state of public feeling on both sides which I thought not favorable to an immediate attempt at renewed negotiations. I accordingly so instructed the minister of the United States to Great Britain, and found that my views in this regard were shared by Her Majesty's ministers. I hope that the time may soon arrive when the two Governments can approach the solution of this momentous question with an appreciation of what is due to the rights, dignity, and honor of each, and with the determination not only to remove the causes of complaint in the past, but to lay the foundation of a broad principle of public law which will prevent future differences and tend to firm and continued peace and friendship.

This is now the only grave question which the United States has with any foreign nation.

The question of renewing a treaty for reciprocal trade between the United States and the British Provinces on this continent has not been favorably considered by the Administration. The advantages of such a treaty would be wholly in favor of the British producer. Except, possibly, a few engaged in the trade between the two sections, no citizen of the United States would be benefited by reciprocity. Our internal taxation would prove a protection to the British producer almost equal to the protection which our manufacturers now receive from the tariff. Some arrangement, however, for the regulation of commercial intercourse between the United States and the Dominion of Canada may be desirable.

The commission for adjusting the claims of the "Hudsons Bay and Puget Sound Agricultural Company" upon the United States has terminated its labors. The award of $650,000 has been made and all rights and titles of the company on the territory of the United States have been extinguished. Deeds for the property of the company have been delivered. An appropriation by Congress to meet this sum is asked.

The commissioners for determining the northwestern land boundary between the United States and the British possessions under the treaty of 1856 have completed their labors, and the commission has been dissolved.

In conformity with the recommendation of Congress, a proposition was early made to the British Government to abolish the mixed courts created under the treaty of April 7, 1862, for the suppression of the slave trade. The subject is still under negotiation.

It having come to my knowledge that a corporate company, organized under British laws, proposed to land upon the shores of the United States and to operate there a submarine cable, under a concession from His Majesty the Emperor of the French of an exclusive right for twenty years of telegraphic communication between the shores of France and the United States, with the very objectionable feature of subjecting all messages conveyed thereby to the scrutiny and control of the French Government, I caused the French and British legations at Washington to be made acquainted with the probable policy of Congress on this subject, as foreshadowed by the bill which passed the Senate in March last. This drew from the representatives of the company an agreement to accept as the basis of their operations the provisions of that bill, or of such other enactment on the subject as might be passed during the approaching session of Congress; also, to use their influence to secure from the French Government a modification of their concession, so as to permit the landing upon French soil of any cable belonging to any company incorporated by the authority of the United States or of any State in the Union, and, on their part, not to oppose the establishment of any such cable. In consideration of this agreement I directed the withdrawal of all opposition by the United States authorities to the landing of the cable and to the working of it until the meeting of Congress. I regret to say that there has been no modification made in the company's concession, nor, so far as I can learn, have they attempted to secure one. Their concession excludes the capital and the citizens of the United States from competition upon the shores of France. I recommend legislation to protect the rights of citizens of the United States, as well as the dignity and sovereignty of the nation, against such an assumption. I shall also endeavor to secure, by negotiation, an abandonment of the principle of monopolies in ocean telegraphic cables. Copies of this correspondence are herewith furnished.

The unsettled political condition of other countries, less fortunate than our own, sometimes induces their citizens to come to the United States for the sole purpose of becoming naturalized. Having secured this, they return to their native country and reside there, without disclosing their change of allegiance. They accept official positions of trust or honor, which can only be held by citizens of their native land; they journey under passports describing them as such citizens; and it is only when civil discord, after perhaps years of quiet, threatens their persons or their property, or when their native state drafts them into its military service, that the fact of their change of allegiance is made known. They reside permanently away from the United States, they contribute nothing to its revenues, they avoid the duties of its citizenship, and they only make themselves known by a claim of protection. I have directed the diplomatic and consular officers of the United States to scrutinize carefully all such claims for protection. The citizen of the United States, whether native or adopted, who discharges his duty to his country, is entitled to its complete protection. While I have a voice in the direction of affairs I shall not consent to imperil this sacred right by conferring it upon fictitious or fraudulent claimants.

On the accession of the present Administration it was found that the minister for North Germany had made propositions for the negotiation of a convention for the protection of emigrant passengers, to which no response had been given. It was concluded that to be effectual all the maritime powers engaged in the trade should join in such a measure. Invitations have been extended to the cabinets of London, Paris, Florence, Berlin, Brussels, The Hague, Copenhagen, and Stockholm to empower their representatives at Washington to simultaneously enter into negotiations and to conclude with the United States conventions identical in form, making uniform regulations as to the construction of the parts of vessels to be devoted to the use of emigrant passengers, as to the quality and quantity of food, as to the medical treatment of the sick, and as to the rules to be observed during the voyage, in order to secure ventilation, to promote health, to prevent intrusion, and to protect the females; and providing for the establishment of tribunals in the several countries for enforcing such regulations by summary process.

Your attention is respectfully called to the law regulating the tariff on Russian hemp, and to the question whether to fix the charges on Russian hemp higher than they are fixed upon manila is not a violation of our treaty with Russia placing her products upon the same footing with those of the most favored nations.

Our manufactures are increasing with wonderful rapidity under the encouragement which they now receive. With the improvements in machinery already effected, and still increasing, causing machinery to take the place of skilled labor to a large extent, our imports of many articles must fall off largely within a very few years. Fortunately, too, manufactures are not confined to a few localities, as formerly, and it is to be hoped will become more and more diffused, making the interest in them equal in all sections. They give employment and support to hundreds of thousands of people at home, and retain with us the means which otherwise would be shipped abroad. The extension of railroads in Europe and the East is bringing into competition with our agricultural products like products of other countries. Self-interest, if not self-preservation, therefore dictates caution against disturbing any industrial interest of the country. It teaches us also the necessity of looking to other markets for the sale of our surplus. Our neighbors south of us and China and Japan, should receive our special attention. It will be the endeavor of the Administration to cultivate such relations with all these nations as to entitle us to their confidence and make it their interest, as well as ours, to establish better commercial relations.

Through the agency of a more enlightened policy than that heretofore pursued toward China, largely due to the sagacity and efforts of one of our own distinguished citizens, the world is about to commence largely increased relations with that populous and hitherto exclusive nation. As the United States have been the initiators in this new policy, so they should be the most earnest in showing their good faith in making it a success. In this connection I advise such legislation as will forever preclude the enslavement of the Chinese upon our soil under the name of coolies, and also prevent American vessels from engaging in the transportation of coolies to any country tolerating the system. I also recommend that the mission to China be raised to one of the first class.

On my assuming the responsible duties of Chief Magistrate of the United States it was with the conviction that three things were essential to its peace, prosperity, and fullest development. First among these is strict integrity in fulfilling all our obligations; second, to secure protection to the person and property of the citizen of the United States in each and every portion of our common country, wherever he may choose to move, without reference to original nationality, religion, color, or politics, demanding of him only obedience to the laws and proper respect for the rights of others; third, union of all the States, with equal rights, indestructible by any constitutional means.

To secure the first of these, Congress has taken two essential steps: First, in declaring by joint resolution that the public debt shall be paid, principal and interest, in coin; and, second, by providing the means for paying. Providing the means, however, could not secure the object desired without a proper administration of the laws for the collection of the revenues and an economical disbursement of them. To this subject the Administration has most earnestly addressed itself, with results, I hope, satisfactory to the country. There has been no hesitation in changing officials in order to secure an efficient execution of the laws, sometimes, too, when, in a mere party view, undesirable political results were likely to follow; nor any hesitation in sustaining efficient officials against remonstrances wholly political.

It may be well to mention here the embarrassment possible to arise from leaving on the statute books the so-called "tenure-of-office acts," and to earnestly recommend their total repeal. It could not have been the intention of the framers of the Constitution, when providing that appointments made by the President should receive the consent of the Senate, that the latter should have the power to retain in office persons placed there by Federal appointment against the will of the President. The law is inconsistent with a faithful and efficient administration of the Government. What faith can an Executive put in officials forced upon him, and those, too, whom he has suspended for reason? How will such officials be likely to serve an Administration which they know does not trust them?

For the second requisite to our growth and prosperity time and a firm but humane administration of existing laws (amended from time to time as they may prove ineffective or prove harsh and unnecessary) are probably all that are required.

The third can not be attained by special legislation, but must be regarded as fixed by the Constitution itself and gradually acquiesced in by force of public opinion.

From the foundation of the Government to the present the management of the original inhabitants of this continent—the Indians—has been a subject of embarrassment and expense, and has been attended with continuous robberies, murders, and wars. From my own experience upon the frontiers and in Indian countries, I do not hold either legislation or the conduct of the whites who come most in contact with the Indian blameless for these hostilities. The past, however, can not be undone, and the question must be met as we now find it. I have attempted a new policy toward these wards of the nation (they can not be regarded in any other light than as wards), with fair results so far as tried, and which I hope will be attended ultimately with great success. The Society of Friends is well known as having succeeded in living in peace with the Indians in the early settlement of Pennsylvania, while their white neighbors of other sects in other sections were constantly embroiled. They are also known for their opposition to all strife, violence, and war, and are generally noted for their strict integrity and fair dealings.

These considerations induced me to give the management of a few reservations of Indians to them and to throw the burden of the selection of agents upon the society itself. The result has proven most satisfactory. It will be found more fully set forth in the report of the Commissioner of Indian Affairs. For superintendents and Indian agents not on the reservations, officers of the Army were selected. The reasons for this are numerous. Where Indian agents are sent, there, or near there, troops must be sent also. The agent and the commander of troops are independent of each other, and are subject to orders from different Departments of the Government. The army officer holds a position for life; the agent, one at the will of the President. The former is personally interested in living in harmony with the Indian and in establishing a permanent peace, to the end that some portion of his life may be spent within the limits of civilized society; the latter has no such personal interest. Another reason is an economic one; and still another, the hold which the Government has upon a life officer to secure a faithful discharge of duties in carrying out a given policy.

The building of railroads, and the access thereby given to all the agricultural and mineral regions of the country, is rapidly bringing civilized settlements into contact with all the tribes of Indians. No matter what ought to be the relations between such settlements and the aborigines, the fact is they do not harmonize well, and one or the other has to give way in the end. A system which looks to the extinction of a race is too horrible for a nation to adopt without entailing upon itself the wrath of all Christendom and engendering in the citizen a disregard for human life and the rights of others, dangerous to society. I see no substitute for such a system, except in placing all the Indians on large reservations, as rapidly as it can be done, and giving them absolute protection there. As soon as they are fitted for it they should be induced to take their lands in severalty and to set up Territorial governments for their own protection. For full details on this subject I call your special attention to the reports of the Secretary of the Interior and the Commissioner of Indian Affairs.

The report of the Secretary of War shows the expenditures of the War Department for the year ending June 30, 1869, to be $80,644,042, of which $23,882,310 was disbursed in the payment of debts contracted during the war, and is not chargeable to current army expenses. His estimate of $34,531,031 for the expenses of the Army for the next fiscal year is as low as it is believed can be relied on. The estimates of bureau officers have been carefully scrutinized, and reduced wherever it has been deemed practicable. If, however, the condition of the country should be such by the beginning of the next fiscal year as to admit of a greater concentration of troops, the appropriation asked for will not be expended.

The appropriations estimated for river and harbor improvements and for fortifications are submitted separately. Whatever amount Congress may deem proper to appropriate for these purposes will be expended.

The recommendation of the General of the Army that appropriations be made for the forts at Boston. Portland, New York, Philadelphia, New Orleans, and San Francisco, if for no other, is concurred in. I also ask your special attention to the recommendation of the general commanding the Military Division of the Pacific for the sale of the seal islands of St. Paul and St. George, Alaska Territory, and suggest that it either be complied with or that legislation be had for the protection of the seal fisheries from which a revenue should be derived.

The report of the Secretary of War contains a synopsis of the reports of the heads of bureaus, of the commanders of military divisions, and of the districts of Virginia, Mississippi, and Texas, and the report of the General of the Army in full. The recommendations therein contained have been well considered, and are submitted for your action. I, however, call special attention to the recommendation of the Chief of Ordnance for the sale of arsenals and lands no longer of use to the Government; also, to the recommendation of the Secretary of War that the act of 3d March, 1869, prohibiting promotions and appointments in the staff corps of the Army, be repealed. The extent of country to be garrisoned and the number of military posts to be occupied is the same with a reduced Army as with a large one. The number of staff officers required is more dependent upon the latter than the former condition.

The report of the Secretary of the Navy accompanying this shows the condition of the Navy when this Administration came into office and the changes made since. Strenuous efforts have been made to place as many vessels "in commission," or render them fit for service if required, as possible, and to substitute the sail for steam while cruising, thus materially reducing the expenses of the Navy and adding greatly to its efficiency. Looking to our future, I recommend a liberal, though not extravagant, policy toward this branch of the public service.

The report of the Postmaster-General furnishes a clear and comprehensive exhibit of the operations of the postal service and of the financial condition of the Post-Office Department. The ordinary postal revenues for the year ending the 30th of June, 1869, amounted to $18,344,510, and the expenditures to $23,698,131, showing an excess of expenditures over receipts of $5,353,620. The excess of expenditures over receipts for the previous year amounted to $6,437,992. The increase of revenues for 1869 over those of 1868 was $2,051,909, and the increase of expenditures was $967,538. The increased revenue in 1869 exceeded the increased revenue in 1868 by $996,336, and the increased expenditure in 1869 was $2,527,570 less than the increased expenditure in 1868, showing by comparison this gratifying feature of improvement, that while the increase of expenditures over the increase of receipts in 1868 was $2,439,535, the increase of receipts over the increase of expenditures in 1869 was $1,084,371.

Your attention is respectfully called to the recommendations made by the Postmaster-General for authority to change the rate of compensation to the main trunk railroad lines for their services in carrying the mails; for having post-route maps executed; for reorganizing and increasing the efficiency of the special-agency service; for increase of the mail service on the Pacific, and for establishing mail service, under the flag of the Union, on the Atlantic; and most especially do I call your attention to his recommendation for the total abolition of the franking privilege. This is an abuse from which no one receives a commensurate advantage; it reduces the receipts for postal service from 25 to 30 per cent and largely increases the service to be performed. The method by which postage should be paid upon public matter is set forth fully in the report of the Postmaster-General.

The report of the Secretary of the Interior shows that the quantity of public lands disposed of during the year ending the 30th of June, 1869, was 7,666,152 acres, exceeding that of the preceding year by 1,010,409 acres. Of this amount 2,899,544 acres were sold for cash and 2,737,365 acres entered under the homestead laws. The remainder was granted to aid in the construction of works of internal improvement, approved to the States as swamp land, and located with warrants and scrip. The cash receipts from all sources were $4,472,886, exceeding those of the preceding year $2,840,140.

During the last fiscal year 23,196 names were added to the pension rolls and 4,876 dropped therefrom, leaving at its close 187,963. The amount paid to pensioners, including the compensation of disbursing agents, was $28,422,884, an increase of $4,411,902 on that of the previous year. The munificence of Congress has been conspicuously manifested in its legislation for the soldiers and sailors who suffered in the recent struggle to maintain "that unity of government which makes us one people." The additions to the pension rolls of each successive year since the conclusion of hostilities result in a great degree from the repeated amendments of the act of the 14th of July, 1862, which extended its provisions to cases not falling within its original scope. The large outlay which is thus occasioned is further increased by the more liberal allowance bestowed since that date upon those who in the line of duty were wholly or permanently disabled. Public opinion has given an emphatic sanction to these measures of Congress, and it will be conceded that no part of our public burden is more cheerfully borne than that which is imposed by this branch of the service. It necessitates for the next fiscal year, in addition to the amount justly chargeable to the naval pension fund, an appropriation of $30,000,000.

During the year ending the 30th of September, 1869, the Patent Office issued 13,762 patents, and its receipts were $686,389, being $213,926 more than the expenditures.

Messages and Papers of the Presidents, Ulysses S. Grant, vol. 6, p.3995

I would respectfully call your attention to the recommendation of the Secretary of the Interior for uniting the duties of supervising the education of freedmen with the other duties devolving upon the Commissioner of Education.

If it is the desire of Congress to make the census which must be taken during the year 1870 more complete and perfect than heretofore, I would suggest early action upon any plan that may be agreed upon. As Congress at the last session appointed a committee to take into consideration such measures as might be deemed proper in reference to the census and report a plan, I desist from saying more.

I recommend to your favorable consideration the claims of the Agricultural Bureau for liberal appropriations. In a country so diversified in climate and soil as ours, and with a population so largely dependent upon agriculture, the benefits that can be conferred by properly fostering this Bureau are incalculable.

I desire respectfully to call the attention of Congress to the inadequate salaries of a number of the most important offices of the Government. In this message I will not enumerate them, but will specify only the justices of the Supreme Court. No change has been made in their salaries for fifteen years. Within that time the labors of the court have largely increased and the expenses of living have at least doubled. During the same time Congress has twice found it necessary to increase largely the compensation of its own members, and the duty which it owes to another department of the Government deserves, and will undoubtedly receive, its due consideration.

There are many subjects not alluded to in this message which might with propriety be introduced, but I abstain, believing that your patriotism and statesmanship will suggest the topics and the legislation most conducive to the interests of the whole people. On my part I promise a rigid adherence to the laws and their strict enforcement.

U. S. GRANT

December 5, 1870
To the Senate and House of Representatives:

A year of peace and general prosperity to this nation has passed since the last assembling of Congress. We have, through a kind Providence, been blessed with abundant crops, and have been spared from complications and war with foreign nations. In our midst comparative harmony has been restored. It is to be regretted, however, that a free exercise of the elective franchise has by violence and intimidation been denied to citizens in exceptional cases in several of the States lately in rebellion, and the verdict of the people has thereby been reversed. The States of Virginia, Mississippi, and Texas have been restored to representation in our national councils. Georgia, the only State now without representation, may confidently be expected to take her place there also at the beginning of the new year, and then, let us hope, will be completed the work of reconstruction. With an acquiescence on the part of the whole people in the national obligation to pay the public debt created as the price of our Union, the pensions to our disabled soldiers and sailors and their widows and orphans, and in the changes to the Constitution which have been made necessary by a great rebellion, there is no reason why we should not advance in material prosperity and happiness as no other nation ever did after so protracted and devastating a war.

Soon after the existing war broke out in Europe the protection of the United States minister in Paris was invoked in favor of North Germans domiciled in French territory. Instructions were issued to grant the protection. This has been followed by an extension of American protection to citizens of Saxony, Hesse and Saxe-Coburg, Gotha, Colombia, Portugal, Uruguay, the Dominican Republic, Ecuador, Chile, Paraguay, and Venezuela in Paris. The charge was an onerous one, requiring constant and severe labor, as well as the exercise of patience, prudence, and good judgment. It has been performed to the entire satisfaction of this Government, and, as I am officially informed, equally so to the satisfaction of the Government of North Germany.

As soon as I learned that a republic had been proclaimed at Paris and that the people of France had acquiesced in the change, the minister of the United States was directed by telegraph to recognize it and to tender my congratulations and those of the people of the United States. The reestablishment in France of a system of government disconnected with the dynastic traditions of Europe appeared to be a proper subject for the felicitations of Americans. Should the present struggle result in attaching the hearts of the French to our simpler forms of representative government, it will be a subject of still further satisfaction to our people. While we make no effort to impose our institutions upon the inhabitants of other countries, and while we adhere to our traditional neutrality in civil contests elsewhere, we can not be indifferent to the spread of American political ideas in a great and highly civilized country like France.

We were asked by the new Government to use our good offices, jointly with those of European powers, in the interests of peace. Answer was made that the established policy and the true interests of the United States forbade them to interfere in European questions jointly with European powers. I ascertained, informally and unofficially, that the Government of North Germany was not then disposed to listen to such representations from any power, and though earnestly wishing to see the blessings of peace restored to the belligerents, with all of whom the United States are on terms of friendship, I declined on the part of this Government to take a step which could only result in injury to our true interests without advancing the object for which our intervention was invoked. Should the time come when the action of the United States can hasten the return of peace by a single hour, that action will be heartily taken. I deemed it prudent, in view of the number of persons of German and French birth living in the United States, to issue, soon after official notice of a state of war had been received from both belligerents, a proclamation defining the duties of the United States as a neutral and the obligations of persons residing within their territory to observe their laws and the laws of nations. This proclamation was followed by others, as circumstances seemed to call for them. The people, thus acquainted in advance of their duties and obligations, have assisted in preventing violations of the neutrality of the United States.

It is not understood that the condition of the insurrection in Cuba has materially changed since the close of the last session of Congress. In an early stage of the contest the authorities of Spain inaugurated a system of arbitrary arrests, of close confinement, and of military trial and execution of persons suspected of complicity with the insurgents, and of summary embargo of their properties, and sequestration of their revenues by executive warrant. Such proceedings, so far as they affected the persons or property of citizens of the United States, were in violation of the provisions of the treaty of 1795 between the United States and Spain.

Representations of injuries resulting to several persons claiming to be citizens of the United States by reason of such violations were made to the Spanish Government. From April, 1869, to June last the Spanish minister at Washington had been clothed with a limited power to aid in redressing such wrongs. That power was found to be withdrawn, "in view," as it was said, "of the favorable situation in which the island of Cuba" then "was," which, however, did not lead to a revocation or suspension of the extraordinary and arbitrary functions exercised by the executive power in Cuba, and we were obliged to make our complaints at Madrid. In the negotiations thus opened, and still pending there, the United States only claimed that for the future the rights secured to their citizens by treaty should be respected in Cuba, and that as to the past a joint tribunal should be established in the United States with full jurisdiction over all such claims. Before such an impartial tribunal each claimant would be required to prove his case. On the other hand, Spain would be at liberty to traverse every material fact, and thus complete equity would be done. A case which at one time threatened seriously to affect the relations between the United States and Spain has already been disposed of in this way. The claim of the owners of the Colonel Lloyd Aspinwall for the illegal seizure and detention of that vessel was referred to arbitration by mutual consent, and has resulted in an award to the United States, for the owners, of the sum of $19,702.50 in gold.

Another and long-pending claim of like nature, that of the whaleship Canada, has been disposed of by friendly arbitrament during the present year. It was referred, by the joint consent of Brazil and the United States, to the decision of Sir Edward Thornton, Her Britannic Majesty's minister at Washington, who kindly undertook the laborious task of examining the voluminous mass of correspondence and testimony submitted by the two Governments, and awarded to the United States the sum of $100,740.09 in gold, which has since been paid by the Imperial Government. These recent examples show that the mode which the United States have proposed to Spain for adjusting the pending claims is just and feasible, and that it may be agreed to by either nation without dishonor. It is to be hoped that this moderate demand may be acceded to by Spain without further delay. Should the pending negotiations, unfortunately and unexpectedly, be without result, it will then become my duty to communicate that fact to Congress and invite its action on the subject.

The long-deferred peace conference between Spain and the allied South American Republics has been inaugurated in Washington under the auspices of the United States. Pursuant to the recommendation contained in the resolution of the House of Representatives of the 17th of December, 1866, the executive department of the Government offered its friendly offices for the promotion of peace and harmony between Spain and the allied Republics. Hesitations and obstacles occurred to the acceptance of the offer. Ultimately, however, a conference was arranged, and was opened in this city on the 29th of October last, at which I authorized the Secretary of State to preside. It was attended by the ministers of Spain, Peru, Chile, and Ecuador. In consequence of the absence of a representative from Bolivia, the conference was adjourned until the attendance of a plenipotentiary from that Republic could be secured or other measures could be adopted toward compassing its objects.

The allied and other Republics of Spanish origin on this continent may see in this fact a new proof of our sincere interest in their welfare, of our desire to see them blessed with good governments, capable of maintaining order and of preserving their respective territorial integrity, and of our sincere wish to extend our own commercial and social relations with them. The time is not probably far distant when, in the natural course of events, the European political connection with this continent will cease. Our policy should be shaped, in view of this probability, so as to ally the commercial interests of the Spanish American States more closely to our own, and thus give the United States all the preeminence and all the advantage which Mr. Monroe, Mr. Adams, and Mr. Clay contemplated when they proposed to join in the congress of Panama.

During the last session of Congress a treaty for the annexation of the Republic of San Domingo to the United States failed to receive the requisite two-thirds vote of the Senate. I was thoroughly convinced then that the best interests of this country, commercially and materially, demanded its ratification. Time has only confirmed me in this view. I now firmly believe that the moment it is known that the United States have entirely abandoned the project of accepting as a part of its territory the island of San Domingo a free port will be negotiated for by European nations in the Bay of Samana. A large commercial city will spring up, to which we will be tributary without receiving corresponding benefits, and then will be seen the folly of our rejecting so great a prize. The Government of San Domingo has voluntarily sought this annexation. It is a weak power, numbering probably less than 120,000 souls, and yet possessing one of the richest territories under the sun, capable of supporting a population of 10,000,000 people in luxury. The people of San Domingo are not capable of maintaining themselves in their present condition, and must look for outside support. They yearn for the protection of our free institutions and laws, our progress and civilization. Shall we refuse them?

The acquisition of San Domingo is desirable because of its geographical position. It commands the entrance to the Caribbean Sea and the Isthmus transit of commerce. It possesses the richest soil, best and most capacious harbors, most salubrious climate, and the most valuable products of the forests, mine, and soil of any of the West India Islands. Its possession by us will in a few years build up a coastwise commerce of immense magnitude, which will go far toward restoring to us our lost merchant marine. It will give to us those articles which we consume so largely and do not produce, thus equalizing our exports and imports. In case of foreign war it will give us command of all the islands referred to, and thus prevent an enemy from ever again possessing himself of rendezvous upon our very coast. At present our coast trade between the States bordering on the Atlantic and those bordering on the Gulf of Mexico is cut into by the Bahamas and the Antilles. Twice we must, as it were, pass through foreign countries to get by sea from Georgia to the west coast of Florida.

San Domingo, with a stable government, under which her immense resources can be developed, will give remunerative wages to tens of thousands of laborers not now upon the island. This labor will take advantage of every available means of transportation to abandon the adjacent islands and seek the blessings of freedom and its sequence—each inhabitant receiving the reward of his own labor. Porto Rico and Cuba will have to abolish slavery, as a measure of self-preservation, to retain their laborers.

San Domingo will become a large consumer of the products of Northern farms and manufactories. The cheap rate at which her citizens can be furnished with food, tools, and machinery will make it necessary that contiguous islands should have the same advantages in order to compete in the production of sugar, coffee, tobacco, tropical fruits, etc. This will open to us a still wider market for our products. The production of our own supply of these articles will cut off more than one hundred millions of our annual imports, besides largely increasing our exports. With such a picture it is easy to see how our large debt abroad is ultimately to be extinguished. With a balance of trade against us (including interest on bonds held by foreigners and money spent by our citizens traveling in foreign lands) equal to the entire yield of the precious metals in this country, it is not so easy to see how this result is to be otherwise accomplished.

The acquisition of San Domingo is an adherence to the "Monroe doctrine;" it is a measure of national protection; it is asserting our just claim to a controlling influence over the great commercial traffic soon to flow from west to east by way of the Isthmus of Darien; it is to build up our merchant marine; it is to furnish new markets for the products of our farms, shops, and manufactories; it is to make slavery insupportable in Cuba and Porto Rico at once, and ultimately so in Brazil; it is to settle the unhappy condition of Cuba and end an exterminating conflict; it is to provide honest means of paying our honest debts without overtaxing the people; it is to furnish our citizens with the necessaries of everyday life at cheaper rates than ever before; and it is, in fine, a rapid stride toward that greatness which the intelligence, industry, and enterprise of the citizens of the United States entitle this country to assume among nations.

In view of the importance of this question, I earnestly urge upon Congress early action expressive of its views as to the best means of acquiring San Domingo. My suggestion is that by joint resolution of the two Houses of Congress the Executive be authorized to appoint a commission to negotiate a treaty with the authorities of San Domingo for the acquisition of that island, and that an appropriation be made to defray the expenses of such a commission. The question may then be determined, either by the action of the Senate upon the treaty or the joint action of the two Houses of Congress upon a resolution of annexation, as in the case of the acquisition of Texas. So convinced am I of the advantages to flow from the acquisition of San Domingo, and of the great disadvantages—I might almost say calamities—to flow from nonacquisition, that I believe the subject has only to be investigated to be approved.

It is to be regretted that our representations in regard to the injurious effects, especially upon the revenue of the United States, of the policy of the Mexican Government in exempting from impost duties a large tract of its territory on our borders have not only been fruitless, but that it is even proposed in that country to extend the limits within which the privilege adverted to has hitherto been enjoyed. The expediency of taking into your serious consideration proper measures for countervailing the policy referred to will, it is presumed, engage your earnest attention.

It is the obvious interest, especially of neighboring nations, to provide against impunity to those who may have committed high crimes within their borders and who may have sought refuge abroad. For this purpose extradition treaties have been concluded with several of the Central American Republics, and others are in progress.

The sense of Congress is desired, as early as may be convenient, upon the proceedings of the commission on claims against Venezuela, as communicated in my messages of March 16, 1869, March 1, 1870, and March 31, 1870. It has not been deemed advisable to distribute any of the money which has been received from that Government until Congress shall have acted on the subject.

The massacres of French and Russian residents at Tien-Tsin, under circumstances of great barbarity, was supposed by some to have been premeditated, and to indicate a purpose among the populace to exterminate foreigners in the Chinese Empire. The evidence fails to establish such a supposition, but shows a complicity between the local authorities and the mob. The Government at Peking, however, seems to have been disposed to fulfill its treaty obligations so far as it was able to do so. Unfortunately, the news of the war between the German States and France reached China soon after the massacre. It would appear that the popular mind became possessed with the idea that this contest, extending to Chinese waters, would neutralize the Christian influence and power, and that the time was coming when the superstitious masses might expel all foreigners and restore mandarin influence. Anticipating trouble from this cause, I invited France and North Germany to make an authorized suspension of hostilities in the East (where they were temporarily suspended by act of the commanders), and to act together for the future protection in China of the lives and properties of Americans and Europeans.

Since the adjournment of Congress the ratifications of the treaty with Great Britain for abolishing the mixed courts for the suppression of the slave trade have been exchanged. It is believed that the slave trade is now confined to the eastern coast of Africa, whence the slaves are taken to Arabian markets.

The ratifications of the naturalization convention between Great Britain and the United States have also been exchanged during the recess, and thus a long-standing dispute between the two Governments has been settled in accordance with the principles always contended for by the United States.

In April last, while engaged in locating a military reservation near Pembina, a corps of engineers discovered that the commonly received boundary line between the United States and the British possessions at that place is about 4,700 feet south of the true position of the forty-ninth parallel, and that the line, when run on what is now supposed to be the true position of that parallel, would leave the fort of the Hudsons Bay Company at Pembina within the territory of the United States. This information being communicated to the British Government, I was requested to consent, and did consent, that the British occupation of the fort of the Hudsons Bay Company should continue for the present. I deem it important, however, that this part of the boundary line should be definitely fixed by a joint commission of the two Governments, and I submit herewith estimates of the expense of such a commission on the part of the United States and recommend that an appropriation be made for that purpose. The land boundary has already been fixed and marked from the summit of the Rocky Mountains to the Georgian Bay. It should now be in like manner marked from the Lake of the Woods to the summit of the Rocky Mountains.

I regret to say that no conclusion has been reached for the adjustment of the claims against Great Britain growing out of the course adopted by that Government during the rebellion. The cabinet of London, so far as its views have been expressed, does not appear to be willing to concede that Her Majesty's Government was guilty of any negligence, or did or permitted any act during the war by which the United States has just cause of complaint. Our firm and unalterable convictions are directly the reverse. I therefore recommend to Congress to authorize the appointment of a commission to take proof of the amount and the ownership of these several claims, on notice to the representative of Her Majesty at Washington, and that authority be given for the settlement of these claims by the United States, so that the Government shall have the ownership of the private claims, as well as the responsible control of all the demands against Great Britain. It can not be necessary to add that whenever Her Majesty's Government shall entertain a desire for a full and friendly adjustment of these claims the United States will enter upon their consideration with an earnest desire for a conclusion consistent with the honor and dignity of both nations.

The course pursued by the Canadian authorities toward the fishermen of the United States during the past season has not been marked by a friendly feeling. By the first article of the convention of 1818 between Great Britain and the United States it was agreed that the inhabitants of the United States should have forever, in common with British subjects, the right of taking fish in certain waters therein defined. In the waters not included in the limits named in the convention (within 3 miles of parts of the British coast) it has been the custom for many years to give to intruding fishermen of the United States a reasonable warning of their violation of the technical rights of Great Britain. The Imperial Government is understood to have delegated the whole or a share of its jurisdiction or control of these inshore fishing grounds to the colonial authority known as the Dominion of Canada, and this semi-independent but irresponsible agent has exercised its delegated powers in an unfriendly way. Vessels have been seized without notice or warning, in violation of the custom previously prevailing, and have been taken into the colonial ports, their voyages broken up, and the vessels condemned. There is reason to believe that this unfriendly and vexatious treatment was designed to bear harshly upon the hardy fishermen of the United States, with a view to political effect upon this Government. The statutes of the Dominion of Canada assume a still broader and more untenable jurisdiction over the vessels of the United States. They authorize officers or persons to bring vessels hovering within 3 marine miles of any of the coasts, bays, creeks, or harbors of Canada into port, to search the cargo, to examine the master on oath touching the cargo and voyage, and to inflict upon him a heavy pecuniary penalty if true answers are not given; and if such a vessel is found "preparing to fish" within 3 marine miles of any of such coasts, bays, creeks, or harbors without a license, or after the expiration of the period named in the last license granted to it, they provide that the vessel, with her tackle, etc., shall be forfeited. It is not known that any condemnations have been made under this statute. Should the authorities of Canada attempt to enforce it, it will become my duty to take such steps as may be necessary to protect the rights of the citizens of the United States.

It has been claimed by Her Majesty's officers that the fishing vessels of the United States have no right to enter the open ports of the British possessions in North America, except for the purposes of shelter and repairing damages, of purchasing wood and obtaining water; that they have no right to enter at the British custom-houses or to trade there except in the purchase of wood and water, and that they must depart within twenty-four hours after notice to leave. It is not known that any seizure of a fishing vessel carrying the flag of the United States has been made under this claim. So far as the claim is founded on an alleged construction of he convention of 1818, it can not be acquiesced in by the United States. It is hoped that it will not be insisted on by Her Majesty's Government.

During the conferences which preceded the negotiation of the convention of 1818 the British commissioners proposed to expressly exclude the fishermen of the United States from "the privilege of carrying on trade with any of His Britannic Majesty's subjects residing within the limits assigned for their use;" and also that it should not be "lawful for the vessels of the United States engaged in said fishery to have on board any goods, wares, or merchandise whatever, except such as may be necessary for the prosecution of their voyages to and from the said fishing grounds: and any vessel of the United States which shall contravene this regulation may be seized, condemned, and confiscated, with her cargo."

This proposition, which is identical with the construction now put upon the language of the convention, was emphatically rejected by the American commissioners, and thereupon was abandoned by the British plenipotentiaries, and Article I, as it stands in the convention, was substituted.

If, however, it be said that this claim is founded on provincial or colonial statutes, and not upon the convention, this Government can not but regard them as unfriendly, and in contravention of the spirit, if not of the letter, of the treaty, for the faithful execution of which the Imperial Government is alone responsible.

Anticipating that an attempt may possibly be made by the Canadian authorities in the coming season to repeat their unneighborly acts toward our fishermen, I recommend you to confer upon the Executive the power to suspend by proclamation the operation of the laws authorizing the transit of goods, wares, and merchandise in bond across the territory of the United States to Canada, and, further, should such an extreme measure become necessary, to suspend the operation of any laws whereby the vessels of the Dominion of Canada are permitted to enter the waters of the United States. A like unfriendly disposition has been manifested on the part of Canada in the maintenance of a claim of right to exclude the citizens of the United States from the navigation of the St. Lawrence. This river constitutes a natural outlet to the ocean for eight States, with an aggregate population of about 17,600,000 inhabitants, and with an aggregate tonnage of 661,367 tons upon the waters which discharge into it. The foreign commerce of our ports on these waters is open to British competition, and the major part of it is done in British bottoms.

If the American seamen be excluded from this natural avenue to the ocean, the monopoly of the direct commerce of the lake ports with the Atlantic would be in foreign hands, their vessels on transatlantic voyages having an access to our lake ports which would be denied to American vessels on similar voyages. To state such a proposition is to refute its justice.

During the Administration of Mr. John Quincy Adams Mr. Clay unanswerably demonstrated the natural right of the citizens of the United States to the navigation of this river, claiming that the act of the congress of Vienna in opening the Rhine and other rivers to all nations showed the judgment of European jurists and statesmen that the inhabitants of a country through which a navigable river passes have a natural right to enjoy the navigation of that river to and into the sea, even though passing through the territories of another power. This right does not exclude the coequal right of the sovereign possessing the territory through which the river debouches into the sea to make such regulations relative to the police of the navigation as may be reasonably necessary; but those regulations should be framed in a liberal spirit of comity, and should not impose needless burdens upon the commerce which has the right of transit. It has been found in practice more advantageous to arrange these regulations by mutual agreement. The United States are ready to make any reasonable arrangement as to the police of the St. Lawrence which may be suggested by Great Britain.

If the claim made by Mr. Clay was just when the population of States bordering on the shores of the Lakes was only 3,400,000, it now derives greater force and equity from the increased population, wealth, production, and tonnage of the States on the Canadian frontier. Since Mr. Clay advanced his argument in behalf of our right the principle for which he contended has been frequently, and by various nations, recognized by law or by treaty, and has been extended to several other great rivers. By the treaty concluded at Mayence in 1831 the Rhine was declared free from the point where it is first navigable into the sea. By the convention between Spain and Portugal concluded in 1835 the navigation of the Douro throughout its whole extent was made free for the subjects of both Crowns. In 1853 the Argentine Confederation by treaty threw open the free navigation of the Parana and the Uruguay to the merchant vessels of all nations. In 1856 the Crimean War was closed by a treaty which provided for the free navigation of the Danube. In 1858 Bolivia by treaty declared that it regarded the rivers Amazon and La Plata, in accordance with fixed principles of national law, as highways or channels opened by nature for the commerce of all nations. In 1859 the Paraguay was made free by treaty, and in December, 1866, the Emperor of Brazil by imperial decree declared the Amazon to be open to the frontier of Brazil to the merchant ships of all nations. The greatest living British authority on this subject, while asserting the abstract right of the British claim, says: It seems difficult to deny that Great Britain may ground her refusal upon strict law, but it is equally difficult to deny, first, that in so doing she exercises harshly an extreme and hard law; secondly, that her conduct with respect to the navigation of the St. Lawrence is in glaring and discreditable inconsistency with her conduct with respect to the navigation of the Mississippi. On the ground that she possessed a small domain in which the Mississippi took its rise, she insisted on the right to navigate the entire volume of its waters. On the ground that she possesses both banks of the St. Lawrence, where it disembogues itself into the sea, she denies to the United States the right of navigation, though about one-half of the waters of Lakes Ontario. Erie, Huron, and Superior, and the whole of Lake Michigan, through which the river flows, are the property of the United States. The whole nation is interested in securing cheap transportation from the agricultural States of the West to the Atlantic Seaboard. To the citizens of those States it secures a greater return for their labor; to the inhabitants of the seaboard it affords cheaper food; to the nation, an increase in the annual surplus of wealth. It is hoped that the Government of Great Britain will see the justice of abandoning the narrow and inconsistent claim to which her Canadian Provinces have urged her adherence.

Our depressed commerce is a subject to which I called your special attention at the last session, and suggested that we will in the future have to look more to the countries south of us, and to China and Japan, for its revival. Our representatives to all these Governments have exerted their influence to encourage trade between the United States and the countries to which they are accredited. But the fact exists that the carrying is done almost entirely in foreign bottoms, and while this state of affairs exists we can not control our due share of the commerce of the world; that between the Pacific States and China and Japan is about all the carrying trade now conducted in American vessels. I would recommend a liberal policy toward that line of American steamers—one that will insure its success, and even increased usefulness.

The cost of building iron vessels, the only ones that can compete with foreign ships in the carrying trade, is so much greater in the United States than in foreign countries that without some assistance from the Government they can not be successfully built here. There will be several propositions laid before Congress in the course of the present session looking to a remedy for this evil. Even if it should be at some cost to the National Treasury, I hope such encouragement will be given as will secure American shipping on the high seas and American shipbuilding at home.

The condition of the archives at the Department of State calls for the early action of Congress. The building now rented by that Department is a frail structure, at an inconvenient distance from the Executive Mansion and from the other Departments, is ill adapted to the purpose for which it is used, has not capacity to accommodate the archives, and is not fireproof. Its remote situation, its slender construction, and the absence of a supply of water in the neighborhood leave but little hope of safety for either the building or its contents in case of the accident of a fire. Its destruction would involve the loss of the rolls containing the original acts and resolutions of Congress, of the historic records of the Revolution and of the Confederation, of the whole series of diplomatic and consular archives since the adoption of the Constitution, and of the many other valuable records and papers left with that Department when it was the principal depository of the governmental archives. I recommend an appropriation for the construction of a building for the Department of State.

I recommend to your consideration the propriety of transferring to the Department of the Interior, to which they seem more appropriately to belong, all powers and duties in relation to the Territories with which the Department of State is now charged by law or usage; and from the Interior Department to the War Department the Pension Bureau, so far as it regulates the payment of soldiers' pensions. I would further recommend that the payment of naval pensions be transferred to one of the bureaus of the Navy Department.

The estimates for the expenses of the Government for the next fiscal year are $18,244,346.01 less than for the current one, but exceed the appropriations for the present year for the same items $8,972,127.56. In this estimate, however, is included $22,338,278.37 for public works heretofore begun under Congressional provision, and of which only so much is asked as Congress may choose to give. The appropriation for the same works for the present fiscal year was $11,984,518.08.

The average value of gold, as compared with national currency, for the whole of the year 1869 was about 134, and for eleven months of 1870 the same relative value has been about 115. The approach to a specie basis is very gratifying, but the fact can not be denied that the instability of the value of our currency is prejudicial to our prosperity, and tends to keep up prices, to the detriment of trade. The evils of a depreciated and fluctuating currency are so great that now, when the premium on gold has fallen so much, it would seem that the time has arrived when by wise and prudent legislation Congress should look to a policy which would place our currency at par with gold at no distant day.

The tax collected from the people has been reduced more than $80,000,000 per annum. By steadiness in our present course there is no reason why in a few short years the national tax gatherer may not disappear from the door of the citizen almost entirely. With the revenue stamp dispensed by postmasters in every community, a tax upon liquors of all sorts and tobacco in all its forms, and by a wise adjustment of the tariff, which will put a duty only upon those articles which we could dispense with, known as luxuries, and on those which we use more of than we produce, revenue enough may be raised after a few years of peace and consequent reduction of indebtedness to fulfill all our obligations. A further reduction of expenses, in addition to a reduction of interest account, may be relied on to make this practicable. Revenue reform, if it means this, has my hearty support. If it implies a collection of all the revenue for the support of the Government, for the payment of principal and interest of the public debt, pensions, etc., by directly taxing the people, then I am against revenue reform, and confidently believe the people are with me. If it means failure to provide the necessary means to defray all the expenses of Government, and thereby repudiation of the public debt and pensions, then I am still more opposed to such kind of revenue reform. Revenue reform has not been defined by any of its advocates to my knowledge, but seems to be accepted as something which is to supply every man's wants without any cost or effort on his part.

A true revenue reform can not be made in a day, but must be the work of national legislation and of time. As soon as the revenue can be dispensed with, all duty should be removed from coffee, tea and other articles of universal use not produced by ourselves. The necessities of the country compel us to collect revenue from our imports. An army of assessors and collectors is not a pleasant sight to the citizen, but that of a tariff for revenue is necessary. Such a tariff, so far as it acts as an encouragement to home production, affords employment to labor at living wages, in contrast to the pauper labor of the Old World, and also in the development of home resources.

Under the act of Congress of the 15th day of July, 1870, the Army has gradually been reduced, so that on the 1st day of January, 1871, the number of commissioned officers and men will not exceed the number contemplated by that law.

The War Department building is an old structure, not fireproof, and entirely inadequate in dimensions to our present wants. Many thousands of dollars are now paid annually for rent of private buildings to accommodate the various bureaus of the Department. I recommend an appropriation for a new War Department building, suited to the present and growing wants of the nation.

The report of the Secretary of War shows a very satisfactory reduction in the expenses of the Army for the last fiscal year. For details you are referred to his accompanying report.

The expenses of the Navy for the whole of the last year—i.e., from December 1, 1869, the date of the last report—are less than $19,000,000, or about $1,000,000 less than they were the previous year. The expenses since the commencement of this fiscal year—i.e., since July 1—show for the five months a decrease of over $2,400,000 from those of the corresponding months last year. The estimates for the current year were $28,205,671.37. Those for next year are $20,683,317, with $955,100 additional for necessary permanent improvements. These estimates are made closely for the mere maintenance of the naval establishment as now is, without much in the nature of permanent improvement. The appropriations made for the last and current years were evidently intended by Congress, and are sufficient only, to keep the Navy on its present footing by the repairing and refitting of our old ships.

This policy must, of course, gradually but surely destroy the Navy, and it is in itself far from economical, as each year that it is pursued the necessity for mere repairs in ships and navy-yards becomes more imperative and more costly, and our current expenses are annually increased for the mere repair of ships, many of which must soon become unsafe and useless. I hope during the present session of Congress to be able to submit to it a plan by which naval vessels can be built and repairs made with great saving upon the present cost.

It can hardly be wise statesmanship in a Government which represents a country with over 5,000 miles of coast line on both oceans, exclusive of Alaska, and containing 40,000,000 progressive people, with relations of every nature with almost every foreign country, to rest with such inadequate means of enforcing any foreign policy, either of protection or redress. Separated by the ocean from the nations of the Eastern Continent, our Navy is our only means of direct protection to our citizens abroad or for the enforcement of any foreign policy.

The accompanying report of the Postmaster-General shows a most satisfactory working of that Department. With the adoption of the recommendations contained therein, particularly those relating to a reform in the franking privilege and the adoption of the "correspondence cards," a self-sustaining postal system may speedily be looked for, and at no distant day a further reduction of the rate of postage be attained.

I recommend authorization by Congress to the Postmaster-General and Attorney-General to issue all commissions to officials appointed through their respective Departments. At present these commissions, where appointments are Presidential, are issued by the State Department. The law in all the Departments of Government, except those of the Post-Office and of Justice, authorizes each to issue its own commissions.

Always favoring practical reforms, I respectfully call your attention to one abuse of long standing which I would like to see remedied by this Congress. It is a reform in the civil service of the country. I would have it go beyond the mere fixing of the tenure of office of clerks and employees who do not require "the advice and consent of the Senate" to make their appointments complete. I would have it govern, not the tenure, but the manner of making all appointments. There is no duty which so much embarrasses the Executive and heads of Departments as that of appointments, nor is there any such arduous and thankless labor imposed on Senators and Representatives as that of finding places for constituents. The present system does not secure the best men, and often not even fit men, for public place. The elevation and purification of the civil service of the Government will be hailed with approval by the whole people of the United States.

Reform in the management of Indian affairs has received the special attention of the Administration from its inauguration to the present day. The experiment of making it a missionary work was tried with a few agencies given to the denomination of Friends, and has been found to work most advantageously. All agencies and superintendencies not so disposed of were given to officers of the Army. The act of Congress reducing the Army renders army officers ineligible for civil positions. Indian agencies being civil offices, I determined to give all the agencies to such religious denominations as had heretofore established missionaries among the Indians, and perhaps to some other denominations who would undertake the work on the same terms—i.e., as a missionary work. The societies selected are allowed to name their own agents, subject to the approval of the Executive, and are expected to watch over them and aid them as missionaries, to Christianize and civilize the Indian, and to train him in the arts of peace. The Government watches over the official acts of these agents, and requires of them as strict an accountability as if they were appointed in any other manner. I entertain the confident hope that the policy now pursued will in a few years bring all the Indians upon reservations, where they will live in houses, and have schoolhouses and churches, and will be pursuing peaceful and self-sustaining avocations, and where they may be visited by the law-abiding white man with the same impunity that he now visits the civilized white settlements. I call your special attention to the report of the Commissioner of Indian Affairs for full information on this subject.

During the last fiscal year 8,095,413 acres of public land were disposed of. Of this quantity 3,698,910.05 acres were taken under the homestead law and 2,159,515.81 acres sold for cash. The remainder was located with military warrants, college or Indian scrip, or applied in satisfaction of grants to railroads or for other public uses. The entries under the homestead law during the last year covered 961,545 acres more than those during the preceding year. Surveys have been vigorously prosecuted to the full extent of the means applicable to the purpose. The quantity of land in market will amply supply the present demand. The claim of the settler under the homestead or the preemption laws is not, however, limited to lands subject to sale at private entry. Any unappropriated surveyed public land may, to a limited amount, be acquired under the former laws if the party entitled to enter under them will comply with the requirements they prescribe in regard to the residence and cultivation. The actual settler's preference right of purchase is even broader, and extends to lands which were unsurveyed at the time of his settlement. His right was formerly confined within much narrower limits, and at one period of our history was conferred only by special statutes. They were enacted from time to time to legalize what was then regarded as an unauthorized intrusion upon the national domain. The opinion that the public lands should be regarded chiefly as a source of revenue is no longer maintained. The rapid settlement and successful cultivation of them are now justly considered of more importance to our well-being than is the fund which the sale of them would produce. The remarkable growth and prosperity of our new States and Territories attest the wisdom of the legislation which invites the tiller of the soil to secure a permanent home on terms within the reach of all. The pioneer who incurs the dangers and privations of a frontier life, and thus aids in laying the foundation of new commonwealths, renders a signal service to his country, and is entitled to its special favor and protection. These laws secure that object and largely promote the general welfare. They should therefore be cherished as a permanent feature of our land system.

Good faith requires us to give full effect to existing grants. The time-honored and beneficent policy of setting apart certain sections of public land for educational purposes in the new States should be continued. When ample provision shall have been made for these objects, I submit as a question worthy of serious consideration whether the residue of our national domain should not be wholly disposed of under the provisions the homestead and preemption laws.

In addition to the swamp and overflowed lands granted to the States in which they are situated, the lands taken under the agricultural-college acts and for internal-improvement purposes under the act of September, 1841, and the acts supplemental thereto, there had been conveyed up to the close of the last fiscal year, by patent or other equivalent title, to States and corporations 27,836,257.63 acres for railways, canals, and wagon roads. It is estimated that an additional quantity of 174,735,523 acres is still due under grants for like uses. The policy of thus aiding the States in building works of internal improvement was inaugurated more than forty years since in the grants to Indiana and Illinois, to aid those States in opening canals to connect the waters of the Wabash with those of Lake Erie and the waters of the Illinois with those of Lake Michigan. It was followed, with some modifications, in the grant to Illinois of alternate sections of public land within certain limits of the Illinois Central Railway. Fourteen States and sundry corporations have received similar subsidies in connection with railways completed or in process of construction. As the reserved sections are rated at the double minimum, the sale of them at the enhanced price has thus in many instances indemnified the Treasury for the granted lands. The construction of some of these thoroughfares has undoubtedly given a vigorous impulse to the development of our resources and the settlement of the more distant portions of the country. It may, however, be well insisted that much of our legislation in this regard has been characterized by indiscriminate and profuse liberality. The United States should not loan their credit in aid of any enterprise undertaken by States or corporations, nor grant lands in any instance, unless the projected work is of acknowledged national importance. I am strongly inclined to the opinion that it is inexpedient and unnecessary to bestow subsidies of either description; but should Congress determine otherwise I earnestly recommend that the right of settlers and of the public be more effectually secured and protected by appropriate legislation.

During the year ending September 30, 1870, there were filed in the Patent Office 19,411 applications for patents, 3,374 caveats, and 160 applications for the extension of patents. Thirteen thousand six hundred and twenty-two patents, including reissues and designs, were issued, 1,010 extended, and 1,089 allowed, but not issued by reason of the nonpayment of the final fees. The receipts of the office during the year were $136,304.29 in excess of its expenditures.

The work of the Census Bureau has been energetically prosecuted. The preliminary report, containing much information of special value and interest, will be ready for delivery during the present session. The remaining volumes will be completed with all the dispatch consistent with perfect accuracy in arranging and classifying the returns. We shall thus at no distant day be furnished with an authentic record of our condition and resources. It will, I doubt not, attest the growing prosperity of the country, although during the decade which has just closed it was so severely tried by the great war waged to maintain its integrity and to secure and perpetuate our free institutions.

During the last fiscal year the sum paid to pensioners, including the cost of disbursement, was $27,780,811.11, and 1,758 bounty-land warrants were issued. At its close 198,686 names were on the pension rolls.

The labors of the Pension Office have been directed to the severe scrutiny of the evidence submitted in favor of new claims and to the discovery of fictitious claims which have been heretofore allowed. The appropriation for the employment of special agents for the investigation of frauds has been judiciously used, and the results obtained have been of unquestionable benefit to the service.

The subjects of education and agriculture are of great interest to the success of our republican institutions, happiness, and grandeur as a nation. In the interest of one a bureau has been established in the Interior Department— the Bureau of Education; and in the interest of the other, a separate Department, that of Agriculture. I believe great general good is to flow from the operations of both these Bureaus if properly fostered. I can not commend to your careful consideration too highly the reports of the Commissioners of Education and of Agriculture, nor urge too strongly such liberal legislation as to secure their efficiency.

In conclusion I would sum up the policy of the Administration to be a thorough enforcement of every law; a faithful collection of every tax provided for; economy in the disbursement of the same; a prompt payment of every debt of the nation; a reduction of taxes as rapidly as the requirements of the country will admit; reductions of taxation and tariff, to be so arranged as to afford the greatest relief to the greatest number; honest and fair dealings with all other peoples, to the end that war, with all its blighting consequences, may be avoided, but without surrendering any right or obligation due to us; a reform in the treatment of Indians and in the whole civil service of the country; and, finally, in securing a pure, untrammeled ballot, where every man entitled to cast a vote may do so, just once at each election, without fear of molestation or proscription on account of his political faith, nativity, of color.

U. S. GRANT

December 4, 1871
To the Senate and House of Representatives:

In addressing my third annual message to the law-making branch of the Government it is gratifying to be able to state that during the past year success has generally attended the effort to execute all laws found upon the statute books. The policy has been not to inquire into the wisdom of laws already enacted, but to learn their spirit and intent and to enforce them accordingly.

The past year has, under a wise Providence, been one of general prosperity to the nation. It has, however, been attended with more than usual chastisements in the loss of life and property by storm and fire. These disasters have served to call forth the best elements of human nature in our country and to develop a friendship for us on the part of foreign nations which goes far toward alleviating the distresses occasioned by these calamities. The benevolent, who have so generously shared their means with the victims of these misfortunes, will reap their reward in the consciousness of having performed a noble act and in receiving the grateful thanks of men, women, and children whose sufferings they have relieved.

The relations of the United States with foreign powers continue to be friendly. The year has been an eventful one in witnessing two great nations, speaking one language and having one lineage, settling by peaceful arbitration disputes of long standing and liable at any time to bring those nations into bloody and costly conflict. An example has thus been set which, if successful in its final issue, may be followed by other civilized nations, and finally be the means of returning to productive industry millions of men now maintained to settle the disputes of nations by the bayonet and the broadside.

I transmit herewith a copy of the treaty alluded to, which has been concluded since the adjournment of Congress with Her Britannic Majesty, and a copy of the protocols of the conferences of the commissioners by whom it was negotiated. This treaty provides methods for adjusting the questions pending between the two nations.

Various questions are to be adjusted by arbitration. I recommend Congress at an early day to make the necessary provision for the tribunal at Geneva and for the several commissioners on the part of the United States called for by the treaty.

His Majesty the King of Italy, the President of the Swiss Confederation, and His Majesty the Emperor of Brazil have each consented, on the joint request of the two powers, to name an arbiter for the tribunal at Geneva. I have caused my thanks to be suitably expressed for the readiness with which the joint request has been complied with, by the appointment of gentlemen of eminence and learning to these important positions.

His Majesty the Emperor of Germany has been pleased to comply with the joint request of the two Governments, and has consented to act as the arbitrator of the disputed water boundary between the United States and Great Britain.

The contracting parties in the treaty have undertaken to regard as between themselves certain principles of public law, for which the United States have contended from the commencement of their history. They have also agreed to bring those principles to the knowledge of the other maritime powers and to invite them to accede to them. Negotiations are going on as to the form of the note by which the invitation is to be extended to the other powers.

I recommend the legislation necessary on the part of the United States to bring into operation the articles of the treaty relating to the fisheries and to the other matters touching the relations of the United States toward the British North American possessions, to become operative so soon as the proper legislation shall be had on the part of Great Britain and its possessions. It is much to be desired that this legislation may become operative before the fishermen of the United States begin to make their arrangements for the coming season.

I have addressed a communication, of which a copy is transmitted herewith, to the governors of New York, Pennsylvania, Ohio, Indiana, Michigan, Illinois, and Wisconsin, urging upon the governments of those States, respectively, the necessary action on their part to carry into effect the object of the article of the treaty which contemplates the use of the canals, on either side, connected with the navigation of the lakes and rivers forming the boundary, on terms of equality, by the inhabitants of both countries. It is hoped that the importance of the object and the benefits to flow therefrom will secure the speedy approval and legislative sanction of the States concerned.

I renew the recommendation for an appropriation for determining the true position of the forty-ninth parallel of latitude where it forms the boundary between the United States and the British North American possessions, between the Lake of the Woods and the summit of the Rocky Mountains. The early action of Congress on this recommendation would put it in the power of the War Department to place a force in the field during the next summer.

The resumption of diplomatic relations between France and Germany has enabled me to give directions for the withdrawal of the protection extended to Germans in France by the diplomatic and consular representatives of the United States in that country. It is just to add that the delicate duty of this protection has been performed by the minister and the consul-general at Paris, and the various consuls in France under the supervision of the latter, with great kindness as well as with prudence and tact. Their course has received the commendation of the German Government, and has wounded no susceptibility of the French.

The Government of the Emperor of Germany continues to manifest a friendly feeling toward the United States, and a desire to harmonize with the moderate and just policy which this Government maintains in its relations with Asiatic powers, as well as with the South American Republics. I have given assurances that the friendly feelings of that Government are fully shared by the United States.

The ratifications of the consular and naturalization conventions with the Austro-Hungarian Empire have been exchanged.

I have been officially informed of the annexation of the States of the Church to the Kingdom of Italy, and the removal of the capital of that Kingdom to Rome. In conformity with the established policy of the United States, I have recognized this change. The ratifications of the new treaty of commerce between the United States and Italy have been exchanged. The two powers have agreed in this treaty that private property at sea shall be exempt from capture in case of war between the two powers. The United States have spared no opportunity of incorporating this rule into the obligation of nations.

The Forty-first Congress, at its third session, made an appropriation for the organization of a mixed commission for adjudicating upon the claims of citizens of the United States against Spain growing out of the insurrection in Cuba. That commission has since been organized. I transmit herewith the correspondence relating to its formation and its jurisdiction. It is to be hoped that this commission will afford the claimants a complete remedy for their injuries.

It has been made the agreeable duty of the United States to preside over a conference at Washington between the plenipotentiaries of Spain and the allied South American Republics, which has resulted in an armistice, with the reasonable assurance of a permanent peace.

The intimate friendly relations which have so long existed between the United States and Russia continue undisturbed. The visit of the third son of the Emperor is a proof that there is no desire on the part of his Government to diminish the cordiality of those relations. The hospitable reception which has been given to the Grand Duke is a proof that on our side we share the wishes of that Government. The inexcusable course of the Russian minister at Washington rendered it necessary to ask his recall and to decline to longer receive that functionary as a diplomatic representative. It was impossible, with self-respect or with a just regard to the dignity of the country, to permit Mr. Catacazy to continue to hold intercourse with this Government after his personal abuse of Government officials, and during his persistent interferences, through various means, with the relations between the United States and other powers. In accordance with my wishes, this Government has been relieved of further intercourse with Mr. Catacazy, and the management of the affairs of the imperial legation has passed into the hands of a gentleman entirely unobjectionable.

With Japan we continue to maintain intimate relations. The cabinet of the Mikado has since the close of the last session of Congress selected citizens of the United States to serve in offices of importance in several departments of Government. I have reason to think that this selection is due to an appreciation of the disinterestedness of the policy which the United States have pursued toward Japan. It is our desire to continue to maintain this disinterested and just policy with China as well as Japan. The correspondence transmitted herewith shows that there is no disposition on the part of this Government to swerve from its established course.

Prompted by a desire to put an end to the barbarous treatment of our shipwrecked sailors on the Korean coast, I instructed our minister at Peking to endeavor to conclude a convention with Korea for securing the safety and humane treatment of such mariners.

Admiral Rodgers was instructed to accompany him with a sufficient force to protect him in case of need.

A small surveying party sent out, on reaching the coast was treacherously attacked at a disadvantage. Ample opportunity was given for explanation and apology for the insult. Neither came. A force was then landed. After an arduous march over a rugged and difficult country, the forts from which the outrages had been committed were reduced by a gallant assault and were destroyed. Having thus punished the criminals, and having vindicated the honor of the flag, the expedition returned, finding it impracticable under the circumstances to conclude the desired convention. I respectfully refer to the correspondence relating thereto, herewith submitted, and leave the subject for such action as Congress may see fit to take.

The Republic of Mexico has not yet repealed the very objectionable laws establishing what is known as the "free zone" on the frontier of the United States. It is hoped that this may yet be done, and also that more stringent measures may be taken by that Republic for restraining lawless persons on its frontiers. I hope that Mexico by its own action will soon relieve this Government of the difficulties experienced from these causes.

Our relations with the various Republics of Central and South America continue, with one exception, to be cordial and friendly.

I recommend some action by Congress regarding the overdue installments under the award of the Venezuelan Claims Commission of 1866. The internal dissensions of this Government present no justification for the absence of effort to meet their solemn treaty obligations.

The ratification of an extradition treaty with Nicaragua has been exchanged. It is a subject for congratulation that the great Empire of Brazil has taken the initiatory step toward the abolition of slavery. Our relations with that Empire, always cordial, will naturally be made more so by this act. It is not too much to hope that the Government of Brazil may hereafter find it for its interest, as well as intrinsically right, to advance toward entire emancipation more rapidly than the present act contemplates.

The true prosperity and greatness of a nation is to be found in the elevation and education of its laborers.

It is a subject for regret that the reforms in this direction which were voluntarily promised by the statesmen of Spain have not been carried out in its West India colonies. The laws and regulations for the apparent abolition of slavery in Cuba and Porto Rico leave most of the laborers in bondage, with no hope of release until their lives become a burden to their employers.

I desire to direct your attention to the fact that citizens of the United States, or persons claiming to be citizens of the United States, are large holders in foreign lands of this species of property, forbidden by the fundamental law of their alleged country. I recommend to Congress to provide by stringent legislation a suitable remedy against the holding, owning or dealing in slaves, or being interested in slave property, in foreign lands, either as owners, hirers, or mortgagors, by citizens of the United States.

It is to be regretted that the disturbed condition of the island of Cuba continues to be a source of annoyance and of anxiety. The existence of a protracted struggle in such close proximity to our own territory, without apparent prospect of an early termination, can not be other than an object of concern to a people who, while abstaining from interference in the affairs of other powers, naturally desire to see every country in the undisturbed enjoyment of peace, liberty, and the blessings of free institutions.

Our naval commanders in Cuban waters have been instructed, in case it should become necessary, to spare no effort to protect the lives and property of bona fide American citizens and to maintain the dignity of the flag.

It is hoped that all pending questions with Spain growing out of the affairs in Cuba may be adjusted in the spirit of peace and conciliation which has hitherto guided the two powers in their treatment of such questions.

To give importance to and to add to the efficiency of our diplomatic relations with Japan and China, and to further aid in retaining the good opinion of those peoples, and to secure to the United States its share of the commerce destined to flow between those nations and the balance of the commercial world, I earnestly recommend that an appropriation be made to support at least four American youths in each of those countries, to serve as a part of the official family of our ministers there. Our representatives would not even then be placed upon an equality with the representatives of

Great Britain and of some other powers. As now situated, our representatives in Japan and China have to depend for interpreters and translators upon natives of those countries who know our language imperfectly, or procure for the occasion the services of employees in foreign business houses or the interpreters to other foreign ministers.

I would also recommend liberal measures for the purpose of supporting the American lines of steamers now plying between San Francisco and Japan and China, and the Australian line—almost our only remaining lines of ocean steamers—and of increasing their services.

The national debt has been reduced to the extent of $86,057, 126.80 during the year, and by the negotiation of national bonds at a lower rate of interest the interest on the public debt has been so far diminished that now the sum to be raised for the interest account is nearly $17,000,000 less than on the 1st of March, 1869. It was highly desirable that this rapid diminution should take place, both to strengthen the credit of the country and to convince its citizens of their entire ability to meet every dollar of liability without bankrupting them. But in view of the accomplishment of these desirable ends: of the rapid development of the resources of the country; its increasing ability to meet large demands, and the amount already paid, it is not desirable that the present resources of the country should continue to be taxed in order to continue this rapid payment. I therefore recommend a modification of both the tariff and internal-tax law. I recommend that all taxes from internal sources be abolished, except those collected from spirituous, vinous, and malt liquors, tobacco in its various forms, and from stamps.

In readjusting the tariff I suggest that a careful estimate be made of the amount of surplus revenue collected under the present laws, after providing for the current expenses of the Government, the interest count, and a sinking fund, and that this surplus be reduced in such a manner as to afford the greatest relief to the greatest number. There are many articles not produced at home, but which enter largely into general consumption through articles which are manufactured at home, such as medicines compounded, etc., etc., from which very little revenue is derived, but which enter into general use. All such articles I recommend to be placed on the "free list." Should a further reduction prove advisable, I would then recommend that it be made upon those articles which can best bear it without disturbing home production or reducing the wages of American labor.

I have not entered into figures, because to do so would be to repeat what will be laid before you in the report of the Secretary of the Treasury. The present laws for collecting revenue pay collectors of customs small salaries, but provide for moieties (shares in all seizures), which, at principal ports of entry particularly, raise the compensation of those officials to a large sum. It has always seemed to me as if this system must at times work perniciously. It holds out an inducement to dishonest men, should such get possession of those offices, to be lax in their scrutiny of goods entered, to enable them finally to make large seizures. Your attention is respectfully invited to this subject.

Continued fluctuations in the value of gold, as compared with the national currency, has a most damaging effect upon the increase and development of the country, in keeping up prices of all articles necessary in everyday life. It fosters a spirit of gambling, prejudicial alike to national morals and the national finances. If the question can be met as to how to get a fixed value to our currency, that value constantly and uniformly approaching par with specie, a very desirable object will be gained.

For the operations of the Army in the past year, the expense of maintaining it, the estimate for the ensuing year, and for continuing seacoast and other improvements conducted under the supervision of the War Department, I refer you to the accompanying report of the Secretary of War.

I call your attention to the provisions of the act of Congress approved March 3, 1869, which discontinues promotions in the staff corps of the Army until provided for by law. I recommend that the number of officers in each grade in the staff corps be fixed, and that whenever the number in any one grade falls below the number so fixed, that the vacancy may be filled by promotion from the grade below. I also recommend that when the office of chief of a corps becomes vacant the place may be filled by selection from the corps in which the vacancy exists.

The report of the Secretary of the Navy shows an improvement in the number and efficiency of the naval force, without material increase in the expense of supporting it. This is due to the policy which has been adopted, and is being extended as fast as our material will admit, of using smaller vessels as cruisers on the several stations. By this means we have been enabled to occupy at once a larger extent of cruising grounds, to visit more frequently the ports where the presence of our flag is desirable, and generally to discharge more efficiently the appropriate duties of the Navy in time of peace, without exceeding the number of men or the expenditure authorized by law.

During the past year the Navy has, in addition to its regular service, supplied the men and officers for the vessels of the Coast Survey, and has completed the surveys authorized by Congress of the isthmuses of Darien and Tehuantepec, and, under like authority, has sent out an expedition, completely furnished and equipped, to explore the unknown ocean of the north.

The suggestions of the report as to the necessity for increasing and improving the materiel of the Navy, and the plan recommended for reducing the personnel of the service to a peace standard, by the gradual abolition of certain grades of officers, the reduction of others, and the employment of some in the service of the commercial marine, are well considered and deserve the thoughtful attention of Congress.

I also recommend that all promotions in the Navy above the rank of captain be by selection instead of by seniority. This course will secure in the higher grades greater efficiency and hold out an incentive to young officers to improve themselves in the knowledge of their profession.

The present cost of maintaining the Navy, its cost compared with that of the preceding year, and the estimates for the ensuing year are contained in the accompanying report of the Secretary of the Navy.

The enlarged receipts of the Post-Office Department, as shown by the accompanying report of the Postmaster-General, exhibit a gratifying increase in that branch of the public service. It is the index of the growth of education and of the prosperity of the people, two elements highly conducive to the vigor and stability of republics. With a vast territory like ours, much of it sparsely populated, but all requiring the services of the mail, it is not at present to be expected that this Department can be made self-sustaining. But a gradual approach to this end from year to year is confidently relied on, and the day is not far distant when the Post-Office Department of the Government will prove a much greater blessing to the whole people than it is now.

The suggestions of the Postmaster-General for improvements in the Department presided over by him are earnestly recommended to you, special attention. Especially do I recommend favorable consideration of the plan for uniting the telegraphic system of the United States with the postal system. It is believed that by such a course the cost of telegraphing could be much reduced, and the service as well, if not better, rendered. It would secure the further advantage of extending the telegraph through portions of the country where private enterprise will not construct it. Commerce, trade, and, above all, the efforts to bring a people widely separated into a community of interest are always benefited by a rapid intercommunication. Education, the groundwork of republican institutions, is encouraged by increasing the facilities to gather speedy news from all parts of the country. The desire to reap the benefit of such improvements will stimulate education. I refer you to the report of the Postmaster-General for full details of the operations of last year and for comparative statements of results with former years.

There has been imposed upon the executive branch of the Government the execution of the act of Congress approved April 20, 1871, and commonly known as the Kuklux law, in a portion of the State of South Carolina. The necessity of the course pursued will be demonstrated by the report of the Committee to Investigate Southern Outrages. Under the provisions of the above act I issued a proclamation calling the attention of the people of the

United States to the same, and declaring my reluctance to exercise any of the extraordinary powers thereby conferred upon me, except in case of imperative necessity, but making known my purpose to exercise such powers whenever it should become necessary to do so for the purpose of securing to all citizens of the United States the peaceful enjoyment of the rights guaranteed to them by the Constitution and the laws.

After the passage of this law information was received from time to time that combinations of the character referred to in this law existed and were powerful in many parts of the Southern States, particularly in certain counties in the State of South Carolina.

Careful investigation was made, and it was ascertained that in nine counties of that State such combinations were active and powerful, embracing a sufficient portion of the citizens to control the local authority, and having, among other things, the object of depriving the emancipated class of the substantial benefits of freedom and of preventing the free political action of those citizens who did not sympathize with their own views. Among their operations were frequent scourgings and occasional assassinations, generally perpetrated at night by disguised persons, the victims in almost all cases being citizens of different political sentiments from their own or freed persons who had shown a disposition to claim equal rights with other citizens. Thousands of inoffensive and well disposed citizens were the sufferers by this lawless violence,

Thereupon, on the 12th of October, 1871, a proclamation was issued, in terms of the law, calling upon the members of those combinations to disperse within five days and to deliver to the marshal or military officers of the United States all arms, ammunition, uniforms, disguises, and other means and implements used by them for carrying out their unlawful purposes.

This warning not having been heeded, on the 17th of October another proclamation was issued, suspending the privileges of the writ of habeas corpus in nine counties in that State.

Direction was given that within the counties so designated persons supposed, upon creditable information, to be members of such unlawful combinations should be arrested by the military forces of the United States and delivered to the marshal, to be dealt with according to law. In two of said counties, York and Spartanburg, many arrests have been made. At the last account the number of persons thus arrested was 168. Several hundred, whose criminality was ascertained to be of an inferior degree, were released for the present. These have generally made confessions of their guilt.

Great caution has been exercised in making these arrests, and, notwithstanding the large number, it is believed that no innocent person is now in custody. The prisoners will be held for regular trial in the judicial tribunals of the United States.

As soon as it appeared that the authorities of the United States were about to take vigorous measures to enforce the law, many persons absconded, and there is good ground for supposing that all of such persons have violated the law. A full report of what has been done under this law will be submitted to Congress by the Attorney-General.

In Utah there still remains a remnant of barbarism, repugnant to civilization, to decency, and to the laws of the United States. Territorial officers, however, have been found who are willing to perform their duty in a spirit of equity and with a due sense of the necessity of sustaining the majesty of the law. Neither polygamy nor any other violation of existing statutes will be permitted within the territory of the United States. It is not with the religion of the self-styled Saints that we are now dealing, but with their practices. They will be protected in the worship of God according to the dictates of their consciences, but they will not be permitted to violate the laws under the cloak of religion.

It may be advisable for Congress to consider what, in the execution of the laws against polygamy, is to be the status of plural wives and their offspring. The propriety of Congress passing an enabling act authorizing the Territorial legislature of Utah to legitimize all children born prior to a time fixed in the act might be justified by its humanity to these innocent children. This is a suggestion only, and not a recommendation.

The policy pursued toward the Indians has resulted favorably, so far as can be judged from the limited time during which it has been in operation. Through the exertions of the various societies of Christians to whom has been intrusted the execution of the policy, and the board of commissioners authorized by the law of April 10, 1869, many tribes of Indians have been induced to settle upon reservations, to cultivate the soil, to perform productive labor of various kinds, and to partially accept civilization. They are being cared for in such a way, it is hoped, as to induce those still pursuing their old habits of life to embrace the only opportunity which is left them to avoid extermination.

I recommend liberal appropriations to carry out the Indian peace policy, not only because it is humane, Christian like, and economical, but because it is right.

I recommend to your favorable consideration also the policy of granting a Territorial government to the Indians in the Indian Territory west of Arkansas and Missouri and south of Kansas. In doing so every right guaranteed to the Indian by treaty should be secured. Such a course might in time be the means of collecting most of the Indians now between the Missouri and the Pacific and south of the British possessions into one Territory or one State. The Secretary of the Interior has treated upon this subject at length, and I commend to you his suggestions.

I renew my recommendation that the public lands be regarded as a heritage to our children, to be disposed of only as required for occupation and to actual settlers. Those already granted have been in great part disposed of in such a way as to secure access to the balance by the hardy settler who may wish to avail himself of them, but caution should be exercised even in attaining so desirable an object.

Educational interest may well be served by the grant of the proceeds of the sale of public lands to settlers. I do not wish to be understood as recommending in the least degree a curtailment of what is being done by the General Government for the encouragement of education.

The report of the Secretary of the Interior submitted with this will give you all the information collected and prepared for publication in regard to the census taken during the year 1870; the operations of the Bureau of Education for the year; the Patent Office; the Pension Office; the Land Office, and the Indian Bureau.

The report of the Commissioner of Agriculture gives the operations of his Department for the year. As agriculture is the groundwork of our prosperity, too much importance can not be attached to the labors of this Department. It is in the hands of an able head, with able assistants, all zealously devoted to introducing into the agricultural productions of the nation all useful products adapted to any of the various climates and soils of our vast territory, and to giving all useful information as to the method of cultivation, the plants, cereals, and other products adapted to particular localities. Quietly but surely the Agricultural Bureau is working a great national good, and if liberally supported the more widely its influence will be extended and the less dependent we shall be upon the products of foreign countries.

The subject of compensation to the heads of bureaus and officials holding positions of responsibility, and requiring ability and character to fill properly, is one to which your attention is invited. But few of the officials receive a compensation equal to the respectable support of a family, while their duties are such as to involve millions of interest. In private life services demand compensation equal to the services rendered; a wise economy would dictate the same rule in the Government service.

I have not given the estimates for the support of Government for the ensuing year, nor the comparative statement between the expenditures for the year just passed and the one just preceding, because all these figures are contained in the accompanying reports or in those presented directly to Congress. These estimates have my approval.

More than six years having elapsed since the last hostile gun was fired between the armies then arrayed against each other—one for the perpetuation, the other for the destruction, of the Union—it may well be considered whether it is not now time that the disabilities imposed by the fourteenth amendment should be removed. That amendment does not exclude the ballot, but only imposes the disability to hold offices upon certain classes. When the purity of the ballot is secure, majorities are sure to elect officers reflecting the views of the majority. I do not see the advantage or propriety of excluding men from office merely because they were before the rebellion of standing and character sufficient to be elected to positions requiring them to take oaths to support the Constitution, and admitting to eligibility those entertaining precisely the same views, but of less standing in their communities. It may be said that the former violated an oath, while the latter did not; the latter did not have it in their power to do so. If they had taken this oath, it can not be doubted they would have broken it as did the former class. If there are any great criminals, distinguished above all others for the part they took in opposition to the Government, they might, in the judgment of Congress, be excluded from such an amnesty.

This subject is submitted for your careful consideration.

The condition of the Southern States is, unhappily, not such as all true patriotic citizens would like to see. Social ostracism for opinion's sake, personal violence or threats toward persons entertaining political views opposed to those entertained by the majority of the old citizens, prevents immigration and the flow of much-needed capital into the States lately in rebellion. It will be a happy condition of the country when the old citizens of these States will take an interest in public affairs, promulgate ideas honestly entertained, vote for men representing their views, and tolerate the same freedom of expression and ballot in those entertaining different political convictions.

Under the provisions of the act of Congress approved February 21, 1871, a Territorial government was organized in the District of Columbia. Its results have thus far fully realized the expectations of its advocates. Under the direction of the Territorial officers, a system of improvements has been inaugurated by means of which Washington is rapidly becoming a city worthy of the nation's capital. The citizens of the District having voluntarily taxed themselves to a large amount for the purpose of contributing to the adornment of the seat of Government, I recommend liberal appropriations on the part of Congress, in order that the Government may bear its just share of the expense of carrying out a judicious system of improvements.

By the great fire in Chicago the most important of the Government buildings in that city were consumed. Those burned had already become inadequate to the wants of the Government in that growing city, and, looking to the near future, were totally inadequate. I recommend, therefore, that an appropriation be made immediately to purchase the remainder of the square on which the burned buildings stood, provided it can be purchased at a fair valuation, or provided that the legislature of Illinois will pass a law authorizing its condemnation for Government purposes; and also an appropriation of as much money as can properly be expended toward the erection of new buildings during this fiscal year.

The number of immigrants ignorant of our laws, habits, etc., coming into our country annually has become so great and the impositions practiced upon them so numerous and flagrant that I suggest Congressional action for their protection. It seems to me a fair subject of legislation by Congress. I can not now state as fully as I desire the nature of the complaints made by immigrants of the treatment they receive, but will endeavor to do so during the session of Congress, particularly if the subject should receive your attention.

It has been the aim of the Administration to enforce honesty and efficiency in all public offices. Every public servant who has violated the trust placed in him has been proceeded against with all the rigor of the law. If bad men have secured places, it has been the fault of the system established by law and custom for making appointments, or the fault of those who recommend for Government positions persons not sufficiently well known to them personally, or who give letters indorsing the characters of office seekers without a proper sense of the grave responsibility which such a course devolves upon them. A civil-service reform which can correct this abuse is much desired. In mercantile pursuits the business man who gives a letter of recommendation to a friend to enable him to obtain credit from a stranger is regarded as morally responsible for the integrity of his friend and his ability to meet his obligations. A reformatory law which would enforce this principle against all indorsers of persons for public place would insure great caution in making recommendations. A salutary lesson has been taught the careless and the dishonest public servant in the great number of prosecutions and convictions of the last two years.

It is gratifying to notice the favorable change which is taking place throughout the country in bringing to punishment those who have proven recreant to the trusts confided to them and in elevating to public office none but those who possess the confidence of the honest and the virtuous, who, it will always be found, comprise the majority of the community in which they live.

In my message to Congress one year ago I urgently recommended a reform in the civil service of the country. In conformity with that recommendation Congress, in the ninth section of "An act making appropriations for sundry civil expenses of the Government, and for other purposes," approved March 3, 1871, gave the necessary authority to the Executive to inaugurate a civil-service reform, and placed upon him the responsibility of doing so. Under the authority of said act I convened a board of gentlemen eminently qualified for the work to devise rules and regulations to effect the needed reform. Their labors are not yet complete, but it is believed that they will succeed in devising a plan that can be adopted to the great relief of the Executive, the heads of Departments, and members of Congress, and which will redound to the true interest of the public service. At all events, the experiment shall have a fair trial.

I have thus hastily summed up the operations of the Government during the last year, and made such suggestions as occur to me to be proper for your consideration. I submit them with a confidence that your combined action will be wise, statesmanlike, and in the best interests of the whole country.

U. S. GRANT

December 2, 1872
To the Senate and House of Representatives:

In transmitting to you this my fourth annual message it is with thankfulness to the Giver of All Good that as a nation we have been blessed for the past year with peace at home, peace abroad, and a general prosperity vouchsafed to but few peoples.

With the exception of the recent devastating fire which swept from the earth with a breath, as it were, millions of accumulated wealth in the city of Boston, there has been no overshadowing calamity within the year to record. It is gratifying to note how, like their fellow-citizens of the city of Chicago under similar circumstances a year earlier, the citizens of Boston are rallying under their misfortunes, and the prospect that their energy and perseverance will overcome all obstacles and show the same prosperity soon that they would had no disaster befallen them. Otherwise we have been free from pestilence, war, and calamities, which often overtake nations; and, as far as human judgment can penetrate the future, no cause seems to exist to threaten our present peace.

When Congress adjourned in June last, a question had been raised by Great Britain, and was then pending, which for a time seriously imperiled the settlement by friendly arbitration of the grave differences between this Government and that of Her Britannic Majesty, which by the treaty of Washington had been referred to the tribunal of arbitration which had met at Geneva, in Switzerland.

The arbitrators, however, disposed of the question which had jeoparded the whole of the treaty and threatened to involve the two nations in most unhappy relations toward each other in a manner entirely satisfactory to this Government and in accordance with the views and the policy which it had maintained.

The tribunal, which had convened at Geneva in December, concluded its laborious session on the 14th day of September last, on which day, having availed itself of the discretionary power given to it by the treaty to award a sum in gross, it made its decision, whereby it awarded the sum of $15,500,000 in gold as the indemnity to be paid by Great Britain to the

United States for the satisfaction of all the claims referred to its consideration.

This decision happily disposes of a long-standing difference between the two Governments, and, in connection with another award, made by the German Emperor under a reference to him by the same treaty, leaves these two Governments without a shadow upon the friendly relations which it is my sincere hope may forever remain equally unclouded.

The report of the agent of the United States appointed to attend the Geneva tribunal, accompanied by the protocols of the proceedings of the arbitrators, the arguments of the counsel of both Governments, the award of the tribunal, and the opinions given by the several arbitrators, is transmitted herewith.

I have caused to be communicated to the heads of the three friendly powers who complied with the joint request made to them under the treaty the thanks of this Government for the appointment of arbitrators made by them respectively, and also my thanks to the eminent personages named by them, and my appreciation of the dignity, patience, impartiality, and great ability with which they discharged their arduous and high functions.

Her Majesty's Government has communicated to me the appreciation by Her Majesty of the ability and indefatigable industry displayed by Mr. Adams, the arbitrator named on the part of this Government during the protracted inquiries and discussions of the tribunal. I cordially unite with Her Majesty in this appreciation.

It is due to the agent of the United States before the tribunal to record my high appreciation of the marked ability, unwearied patience, and the prudence and discretion with which he has conducted the very responsible and delicate duties committed to him, as it is also due to the learned and eminent counsel who attended the tribunal on the part of this Government to express my sense of the talents and wisdom which they brought to bear in the attainment of the result so happily reached.

It will be the province of Congress to provide for the distribution among those who may be entitled to it of their respective shares of the money to be paid. Although the sum awarded is not payable until a year from the date of the award, it is deemed advisable that no time be lost in making a proper examination of the several cases in which indemnification may be due. I consequently recommend the creation of a board of commissioners for the purpose.

By the thirty-fourth article of the treaty of Washington the respective claims of the United States and of Great Britain in their construction of the treaty of the 15th of June, 1846, defining the boundary line between their respective territories, were submitted to the arbitration and award of His Majesty the Emperor of Germany, to decide which of those claims is most in accordance with the true interpretation of the treaty of 1846.

His Majesty the Emperor of Germany, having been pleased to undertake the arbitration, has the earnest thanks of this Government and of the people of the United States for the labor, pains, and care which he has devoted to the consideration of this long-pending difference. I have caused an expression of my thanks to be communicated to His Majesty. Mr. Bancroft, the representative of this Government at Berlin, conducted the case and prepared the statement on the part of the United States with the ability that his past services justified the public in expecting at his hands. As a member of the Cabinet at the date of the treaty which has given rise to the discussion between the two Governments, as the minister to Great Britain when the construction now pronounced unfounded was first advanced, and as the agent and representative of the Government to present the case and to receive the award, he has been associated with the question in all of its phases, and in every stage has manifested a patriotic zeal and earnestness in maintenance of the claim of the United States. He is entitled to much credit for the success which has attended the submission.

After a patient investigation of the case and of the statements of each party, His Majesty the Emperor, on the 21st day of October last, signed his award in writing, decreeing that the claim of the Government of the United States, that the boundary line between the territories of Her Britannic Majesty and the United States should be drawn through the Haro Channel, is most in accordance with the true interpretation of the treaty concluded on the 15th of June, 1846, between the Governments of Her Britannic Majesty and of the United States.

Copies of the "case" presented on behalf of each Government, and of the "statement in reply" of each, and a translation of the award, are transmitted herewith.

This award confirms the United States in their claim to the important archipelago of islands lying between the continent and Vancouvers Island, which for more than twenty-six years (ever since the ratification of the treaty) Great Britain has contested, and leaves us, for the first time in the history of the United States as a nation, without a question of disputed boundary between our territory and the possessions of Great Britain on this continent.

It is my grateful duty to acknowledge the prompt, spontaneous action of Her Majesty's Government in giving effect to the award. In anticipation of any request from this Government, and before the reception in the United States of the award signed by the Emperor, Her Majesty had given instructions for the removal of her troops which had been stationed there and for the cessation of all exercise or claim of jurisdiction, so as to leave the United States in the exclusive possession of the lately disputed territory. I am gratified to be able to announce that the orders for the removal of the troops have been executed, and that the military joint occupation of San

Juan has ceased. The islands are now in the exclusive possession of the United States.

It now becomes necessary to complete the survey and determination of that portion of the boundary line (through the Haro Channel) upon which the commission which determined the remaining part of the line were unable to agree. I recommend the appointment of a commission to act jointly with one which may be named by Her Majesty for that purpose.

Experience of the difficulties attending the determination of our admitted line of boundary, after the occupation of the territory and its settlement by those owing allegiance to the respective Governments, points to the importance of establishing, by natural objects or other monuments, the actual line between the territory acquired by purchase from Russia and the adjoining possessions of Her Britannic Majesty. The region is now so sparsely occupied that no conflicting interests of individuals or of jurisdiction are likely to interfere to the delay or embarrassment of the actual location of the line. If deferred until population shall enter and occupy the territory, some trivial contest of neighbors may again array the two Governments in antagonism. I therefore recommend the appointment of a commission, to act jointly with one that may be appointed on the part of Great Britain, to determine the line between our Territory of Alaska and the conterminous possessions of Great Britain.

In my last annual message I recommended the legislation necessary on the part of the United States to bring into operation the articles of the treaty of Washington of May 8, 1871, relating to the fisheries and to other matters touching the relations of the United States toward the British North American possessions, to become operative so soon as the proper legislation should be had on the part of Great Britain and its possessions.

That legislation on the part of Great Britain and its possessions had not then been had, and during the session of Congress a question was raised which for the time raised a doubt whether any action by Congress in the direction indicated would become important. This question has since been disposed of, and I have received notice that the Imperial Parliament and the legislatures of the provincial governments have passed laws to carry the provisions of the treaty on the matters referred to into operation. I therefore recommend your early adoption of the legislation in the same direction necessary on the part of this Government.

The joint commission for determining the boundary line between the United States and the British possessions between the Lake of the Woods and the Rocky Mountains has organized and entered upon its work. It is desirable that the force be increased, in order that the completion of the survey and determination of the line may be the sooner attained. To this end I recommend that a sufficient appropriation be made.

With France, our earliest ally; Russia, the constant and steady friend of the

United States; Germany, with whose Government and people we have so many causes of friendship and so many common sympathies, and the other powers of Europe, our relations are maintained on the most friendly terms. Since my last annual message the exchange has been made of the ratifications of a treaty with the Austro-Hungarian Empire relating to naturalization; also of a treaty with the German Empire respecting consuls and trade-marks; also of a treaty with Sweden and Norway relating to naturalization; all of which treaties have been duly proclaimed.

Congress at its last session having made an appropriation to defray the expense of commissioners on the part of the United States to the International Statistical Congress at St. Petersburg, the persons appointed in that character proceeded to their destination and attended the sessions of the congress. Their report shall in due season be laid before you. This congress meets at intervals of about three years, and has held its sessions in several of the countries of Europe. I submit to your consideration the propriety of extending an invitation to the congress to hold its next meeting in the United States. The Centennial Celebration to be held in 1876 would afford an appropriate occasion for such meeting.

Preparations are making for the international exposition to be held during the next year in Vienna, on a scale of very great magnitude. The tendency of these expositions is in the direction of advanced civilization, and of the elevation of industry and of labor, and of the increase of human happiness, as well as of greater intercourse and good will between nations. As this exposition is to be the first which will have been held in eastern Europe, it is believed that American inventors and manufacturers will be ready to avail themselves of the opportunity for the presentation of their productions if encouraged by proper aid and protection.

At the last session of Congress authority was given for the appointment of one or more agents to represent this Government at the exposition. The authority thus given has been exercised, but, in the absence of any appropriation, there is danger that the important benefits which the occasion offers will in a large degree be lost to citizens of the United States. I commend the subject strongly to your consideration, and recommend that an adequate appropriation be made for the purpose.

To further aid American exhibitors at the Vienna Exposition, I would recommend, in addition to an appropriation of money, that the Secretary of the Navy be authorized to fit up two naval vessels to transport between our Atlantic cities and Trieste, or the most convenient port to Vienna, and back, their articles for exhibition.

Since your last session the President of the Mexican Republic, distinguished by his high character and by his services to his country, has died. His temporary successor has now been elected with great unanimity by the people a proof of confidence on their part in his patriotism and wisdom which it is believed will be confirmed by the results of his administration. It is particularly desirable that nothing should be left undone by the Government of either Republic to strengthen their relations as neighbors and friends.

It is much to be regretted that many lawless acts continue to disturb the quiet of the settlements on the border between our territory and that of Mexico, and that complaints of wrongs to American citizens in various parts of the country are made. The revolutionary condition in which the neighboring Republic has so long been involved has in some degree contributed to this disturbance. It is to be hoped that with a more settled rule of order through the Republic, which may be expected from the present Government, the acts of which just complaint is made will cease.

The proceedings of the commission under the convention with Mexico of the 4th of July, 1868, on the subject of claims, have, unfortunately, been checked by an obstacle, for the removal of which measures have been taken by the two Governments which it is believed will prove successful.

The commissioners appointed, pursuant to the joint resolution of Congress of the 7th of May last, to inquire into depredations on the Texan frontier have diligently made investigations in that quarter. Their report upon the subject will be communicated to you. Their researches were necessarily incomplete, partly on account of the limited appropriation made by Congress. Mexico, on the part of that Government, has appointed a similar commission to investigate these outrages. It is not announced officially, but the press of that country states that the fullest investigation is desired, and that the cooperation of all parties concerned is invited to secure that end. I therefore recommend that a special appropriation be made at the earliest day practicable, to enable the commissioners on the part of the United States to return to their labors without delay.

It is with regret that I have again to announce a continuance of the disturbed condition of the island of Cuba. No advance toward the pacification of the discontented part of the population has been made. While the insurrection has gained no advantages and exhibits no more of the elements of power or of the prospects of ultimate success than were exhibited a year ago, Spain, on the other hand, has not succeeded in its repression, and the parties stand apparently in the same relative attitude which they have occupied for a long time past.

This contest has lasted now for more than four years. Were its scene at a distance from our neighborhood, we might be indifferent to its result, although humanity could not be unmoved by many of its incidents wherever they might occur. It is, however, at our door.

I can not doubt that the continued maintenance of slavery in Cuba is among the strongest inducements to the continuance of this strife. A terrible wrong is the natural cause of a terrible evil. The abolition of slavery and the introduction of other reforms in the administration of government in Cuba could not fail to advance the restoration of peace and order. It is greatly to be hoped that the present liberal Government of Spain will voluntarily adopt this view.

The law of emancipation, which was passed more than two years since, has remained unexecuted in the absence of regulations for its enforcement. It was but a feeble step toward emancipation, but it was the recognition of right, and was hailed as such, and exhibited Spain in harmony with sentiments of humanity and of justice and in sympathy with the other powers of the Christian and civilized world.

Within the past few weeks the regulations for carrying out the law of emancipation have been announced, giving evidence of the sincerity of intention of the present Government to carry into effect the law of 1870. I have not failed to urge the consideration of the wisdom, the policy, and the justice of a more effective system for the abolition of the great evil which oppresses a race and continues a bloody and destructive contest close to our border, as well as the expediency and the justice of conceding reforms of which the propriety is not questioned.

Deeply impressed with the conviction that the continuance of slavery is one of the most active causes of the continuance of the unhappy condition in Cuba, I regret to believe that citizens of the United States, or those claiming to be such, are large holders in Cuba of what is there claimed as property, but which is forbidden and denounced by the laws of the United States. They are thus, in defiance of the spirit of our own laws, contributing to the continuance of this distressing and sickening contest. In my last annual message I referred to this subject, and I again recommend such legislation as may be proper to denounce, and, if not prevent, at least to discourage American citizens from holding or dealing in slaves.

It is gratifying to announce that the ratifications of the convention concluded under the auspices of this Government between Spain on the one part and the allied Republics of the Pacific on the other, providing for an armistice, have been exchanged. A copy of the instrument is herewith submitted. It is hoped that this may be followed by a permanent peace between the same parties.

The differences which at one time threatened the maintenance of peace between Brazil and the Argentine Republic it is hoped are in the way of satisfactory adjustment.

With these States, as with the Republics of Central and of South America, we continue to maintain the most friendly relations.

It is with regret, however, I announce that the Government of Venezuela has made no further payments on account of the awards under the convention of the 25th of April, 1866. That Republic is understood to be now almost, if not quite, tranquilized. It is hoped, therefore, that it will lose no time in providing for the unpaid balance of its debt to the United States, which, having originated in injuries to our citizens by Venezuelan authorities, and having been acknowledged, pursuant to a treaty, in the most solemn form known among nations, would seem to deserve a preference over debts of a different origin and contracted in a different manner. This subject is again recommended to the attention of Congress for such action as may be deemed proper.

Our treaty relations with Japan remain unchanged. An imposing embassy from that interesting and progressive nation visited this country during the year that is passing, but, being unprovided with powers for the signing of a convention in this country, no conclusion in that direction was reached. It is hoped, however, that the interchange of opinions which took place during their stay in this country has led to a mutual appreciation of the interests which may be promoted when the revision of the existing treaty shall be undertaken.

In this connection I renew my recommendation of one year ago, that—

To give importance to and to add to the efficiency of our diplomatic relations with Japan and China, and to further aid in retaining the good opinion of those peoples, and to secure to the United States its share of the commerce destined to flow between those nations and the balance of the commercial world, an appropriation be made to support at least four American youths in each of those countries, to serve as a part of the official family of our ministers there. Our representatives would not even then be placed upon an equality with the representatives of Great Britain and of some other powers. As now situated, our representatives in Japan and China have to depend for interpreters and translators upon natives of those countries, who know our language imperfectly, or procure for the occasion the services of employees in foreign business houses or the interpreters to other foreign ministers.

I renew the recommendation made on a previous occasion, of the transfer to the Department of the Interior, to which they seem more appropriately to belong, of all the powers and duties in relation to the Territories with which the Department of State is now charged by law or by custom.

Congress from the beginning of the Government has wisely made provision for the relief of distressed seamen in foreign countries. No similar provision, however, has hitherto been made for the relief of citizens in distress abroad other than seamen. It is understood to be customary with other governments to authorize consuls to extend such relief to their citizens or subjects in certain cases. A similar authority and an appropriation to carry it into effect are recommended in the case of citizens of the United States destitute or sick under such circumstances. It is well known that such citizens resort to foreign countries in great numbers. Though most of them are able to bear the expenses incident to locomotion, there are some who, through accident or otherwise, become penniless, and have no friends at home able to succor them. Persons in this situation must either perish, cast themselves upon the charity of foreigners, or be relieved at the private charge of our own officers, who usually, even with the most benevolent dispositions, have nothing to spare for such purposes.

Should the authority and appropriation asked for be granted, care will be taken so to carry the beneficence of Congress into effect that it shall not be unnecessarily or unworthily bestowed. TREASURY.

The moneys received and covered into the Treasury during the fiscal year ended June 30, 1872, were:

From customs - $216,370,286.77
From sales of public lands - 2,575,714.19
From internal revenue - 130,642,177.72
From tax on national-bank circulation, etc - 6,523,396.39
From Pacific railway companies - 749,861.87
From customs fines, etc - 1,136,442.34
From fees—consular, patent, lands, etc - 2,284,095.92
From miscellaneous - 412,254.71 -

December 1, 1873
To the Senate and House of Representatives:

The year that has passed since the submission of my last message to Congress has, especially during the latter part of it, been an eventful one to the country. In the midst of great national prosperity a financial crisis has occurred that has brought low fortunes of gigantic proportions; political partisanship has almost ceased to exist, especially in the agricultural regions; and, finally, the capture upon the high seas of a vessel bearing our flag has for a time threatened the most serious consequences, and has agitated the public mind from one end of the country to the other. But this, happily, now is in the course of satisfactory adjustment, honorable to both nations concerned.

The relations of the United States, however, with most of the other powers continue to be friendly and cordial. With France, Germany, Russia, Italy, and the minor European powers; with Brazil and most of the South American Republics, and with Japan, nothing has occurred during the year to demand special notice. The correspondence between the Department of State and various diplomatic representatives in or from those countries is transmitted herewith.

In executing the will of Congress, as expressed in its joint resolution of the 14th of February last, and in accordance with the provisions of the resolution, a number of "practical artisans," of "scientific men," and of "honorary commissioners" were authorized to attend the exposition at

Vienna as commissioners on the part of the United States. It is believed that we have obtained the object which Congress had in view when it passed the joint resolution—"in order to enable the people of the United States to participate in the advantages of the International Exhibition of the Products of Agriculture, Manufactures, and the Fine Arts to be held at Vienna." I take pleasure in adding that the American exhibitors have received a gratifying number of diplomas and of medals.

During the exposition a conference was held at Vienna for the purpose of consultation on the systems prevailing in different countries for the protection of inventions. I authorized a representative from the Patent Office to be present at Vienna at the time when this conference was to take place, in order to aid as far as he might in securing any possible additional protection to American inventors in Europe. The report of this agent will be laid before Congress.

It is my pleasant duty to announce to Congress that the Emperor of China, on attaining his majority, received the diplomatic representatives of the Western powers in person. An account of these ceremonies and of the interesting discussions which preceded them will be found in the documents transmitted herewith. The accompanying papers show that some advance, although slight, has been made during the past year toward the suppression of the infamous Chinese cooly trade. I recommend Congress to inquire whether additional legislation be not needed on this subject.

The money awarded to the United States by the tribunal of arbitration at Geneva was paid by Her Majesty's Government a few days in advance of the time when it would have become payable according to the terms of the treaty. In compliance with the provisions of the act of March 3, 1873, it was at once paid into the Treasury, and used to redeem, so far as it might, the public debt of the United States; and the amount so redeemed was invested in a 5 per cent registered bond of the United States for $15,500,000, which is now held by the Secretary of State, subject to the future disposition of Congress.

I renew my recommendation, made at the opening of the last session of Congress, that a commission be created for the purpose of auditing and determining the amounts of the several "direct losses growing out of the destruction of vessels and their cargoes" by the Alabama, the Florida, or the Shenandoah after leaving Melbourne, for which the sufferers have received no equivalent or compensation, and of ascertaining the names of the persons entitled to receive compensation for the same, making the computations upon the basis indicated by the tribunal of arbitration at Geneva; and that payment of such losses be authorized to an extent not to exceed the awards of the tribunal at Geneva.

By an act approved on the 14th day of February last Congress made provision for completing, jointly with an officer or commissioner to be named by Her Britannic Majesty, the determination of so much of the boundary line between the territory of the United States and the possessions of Great Britain as was left uncompleted by the commissioners appointed under the act of Congress of August 11, 1856. Under the provisions of this act the northwest water boundary of the United States has been determined and marked in accordance with the award of the Emperor of Germany. A protocol and a copy of the map upon which the line was thus marked are contained in the papers submitted herewith.

I also transmit a copy of the report of the commissioner for marking the northern boundary between the United States and the British possessions west of the Lake of the Woods, of the operations of the commission during the past season. Surveys have been made to a point 497 miles west of the Lake of the Woods, leaving about 350 miles to be surveyed, the field work of which can be completed during the next season.

The mixed commission organized under the provisions of the treaty of Washington for settling and determining the claims of citizens of either power against the other arising out of acts committed against their persons or property during the period between April 13, 1861, and April 9, 1865, made its final award on the 25th day of September last. It was awarded that the Government of the United States should pay to the Government of Her Britannic Majesty, within twelve months from the date of the award, the sum of $1,929,819 in gold. The commission disallowed or dismissed all other claims of British subjects against the United States. The amount of the claims presented by the British Government, but disallowed or dismissed, is understood to be about $93,000,000. It also disallowed all the claims of citizens of the United States against Great Britain which were referred to it.

I recommend the early passage of an act appropriating the amount necessary to pay this award against the United States.

I have caused to be communicated to the Government of the King of Italy the thanks of this Government for the eminent services rendered by Count Corti as the third commissioner on this commission. With dignity, learning, and impartiality he discharged duties requiring great labor and constant patience, to the satisfaction, I believe, of both Governments. I recommend legislation to create a special court, to consist of three judges, who shall be empowered to hear and determine all claims of aliens upon the United States arising out of acts committed against their persons or property during the insurrection. The recent reference under the treaty of Washington was confined to claims of British subjects arising during the period named in the treaty; but it is understood that there are other British claims of a similar nature, arising after the 9th of April, 1865, and it is known that other claims of a like nature are advanced by citizens or subjects of other powers. It is desirable to have these claims also examined and disposed of.

Official information being received from the Dutch Government of a state of war between the King of the Netherlands and the Sultan of Acheen, the officers of the United States who were near the seat of the war were instructed to observe an impartial neutrality. It is believed that they have done so.

The joint commission under the convention with Mexico of 1868, having again been legally prolonged, has resumed its business, which, it is hoped, may be brought to an early conclusion. The distinguished representative of Her Britannic Majesty at Washington has kindly consented, with the approval of his Government, to assume the arduous and responsible duties of umpire in this commission, and to lend the weight of his character and name to such decisions as may not receive the acquiescence of both the arbitrators appointed by the respective Governments.

The commissioners appointed pursuant to the authority of Congress to examine into the nature and extent of the forays by trespassers from that country upon the herds of Texas have made a report, which will be submitted for your consideration.

The Venezuelan Government has been apprised of the sense of Congress in regard to the awards of the joint commission under the convention of 25th April, 1866, as expressed in the act of the 25th of February last.

It is apprehended that that Government does not realize the character of its obligations under that convention. As there is reason to believe, however, that its hesitancy in recognizing them springs, in part at least, from real difficulty in discharging them in connection with its obligations to other governments, the expediency of further forbearance on our part is believed to be worthy of your consideration.

The Ottoman Government and that of Egypt have latterly shown a disposition to relieve foreign consuls of the judicial powers which heretofore they have exercised in the Turkish dominions, by organizing other tribunals. As Congress, however, has by law provided for the discharge of judicial functions by consuls of the United States in that quarter under the treaty of 1830, I have not felt at liberty formally to accept the proposed change without the assent of Congress, whose decision upon the subject at as early a period as may be convenient is earnestly requested.

I transmit herewith, for the consideration and determination of Congress, an application of the Republic of Santo Domingo to this Government to exercise a protectorate over that Republic.

Since the adjournment of Congress the following treaties with foreign powers have been proclaimed: A naturalization convention with Denmark; a convention with Mexico for renewing the Claims Commission; a convention of friendship, commerce, and extradition with the Orange Free State, and a naturalization convention with Ecuador.

I renew the recommendation made in my message of December, 1870, that Congress authorize the Postmaster-General to issue all commissions to officials appointed through his Department.

I invite the earnest attention of Congress to the existing laws of the United States respecting expatriation and the election of nationality by individuals. Many citizens of the United States reside permanently abroad with their families. Under the provisions of the act approved February 10, 1855, the children of such persons are to be deemed and taken to be citizens of the United States, but the rights of citizenship are not to descend to persons whose fathers never resided in the United States.

It thus happens that persons who have never resided within the United States have been enabled to put forward a pretension to the protection of the United States against the claim to military service of the government under whose protection they were born and have been reared. In some cases even naturalized citizens of the United States have returned to the land of their birth, with intent to remain there, and their children, the issue of a marriage contracted there after their return, and who have never been in the United States, have laid claim to our protection when the lapse of many years had imposed upon them the duty of military service to the only government which had ever known them personally.

Until the year 1868 it was left, embarrassed by conflicting opinions of courts and of jurists, to determine how far the doctrine of perpetual allegiance derived from our former colonial relations with Great Britain was applicable to American citizens. Congress then wisely swept these doubts away by enacting that—Any declaration, instruction, opinion, order, or decision of any officer of this Government which denies, restricts, impairs, or questions the right of expatriation is inconsistent with the fundamental principles of this Government. But Congress did not indicate in that statute, nor has it since done so, what acts are to be deemed to work expatriation. For my own guidance in determining such questions I required (under the provisions of the Constitution) the opinion in writing of the principal officer in each of the Executive Departments upon certain questions relating to this subject. The result satisfies me that further legislation has become necessary. I therefore commend the subject to the careful consideration of Congress, and I transmit herewith copies of the several opinions of the principal officers of the Executive Departments, together with other correspondence and pertinent information on the same subject.

The United States, who led the way in the overthrow of the feudal doctrine of perpetual allegiance, are among the last to indicate how their own citizens may elect another nationality. The papers submitted herewith indicate what is necessary to place us on a par with other leading nations in liberality of legislation on this international question. We have already in our treaties assented to the principles which would need to be embodied in laws intended to accomplish such results. We have agreed that citizens of the United States may cease to be citizens and may voluntarily render allegiance to other powers. We have agreed that residence in a foreign land, without intent to return, shall of itself work expatriation. We have agreed in some instances upon the length of time necessary for such continued residence to work a presumption of such intent. I invite Congress now to mark out and define when and how expatriation can be accomplished; to regulate by law the condition of American women marrying foreigners; to fix the status of children born in a foreign country of American parents residing more or less permanently abroad, and to make rules for determining such other kindred points as may seem best to Congress.

In compliance with the request of Congress, I transmitted to the American minister at Madrid, with instructions to present it to the Spanish Government, the joint resolution approved on the 3d of March last, tendering to the people of Spain, in the name and on the behalf of the American people, the congratulations of Congress upon the efforts to consolidate in Spain the principles of universal liberty in a republican form of government.

The existence of this new Republic was inaugurated by striking the fetters from the slaves in Porto Rico. This beneficent measure was followed by the release of several thousand persons illegally held as slaves in Cuba. Next, the Captain-General of that colony was deprived of the power to set aside the orders of his superiors at Madrid, which had pertained to the office since 1825. The sequestered estates of American citizens, which had been the cause of long and fruitless correspondence, were ordered to be restored to their owners. All these liberal steps were taken in the face of a violent opposition directed by the reactionary slave-holders of Havana, who are vainly striving to stay the march of ideas which has terminated slavery in Christendom, Cuba only excepted. Unhappily, however, this baneful influence has thus far succeeded in defeating the efforts of all liberal-minded men in Spain to abolish slavery in Cuba, and in preventing the promised reform in that island. The struggle for political supremacy continues there.

The proslavery and aristocratic party in Cuba is gradually arraigning itself in more and more open hostility and defiance of the home government, while it still maintains a political connection with the Republic in the peninsula; and although usurping and defying the authority of the home government whenever such usurpation or defiance tends in the direction of oppression or of the maintenance of abuses, it is still a power in Madrid, and is recognized by the Government. Thus an element more dangerous to continued colonial relations between Cuba and Spain than that which inspired the insurrection at Yara—an element opposed to granting any relief from misrule and abuse, with no aspirations after freedom, commanding no sympathies in generous breasts, aiming to rivet still stronger the shackles of slavery and oppression—has seized many of the emblems of power in Cuba, and, under professions of loyalty to the mother country, is exhausting the resources of the island, and is doing acts which are at variance with those principles of justice, of liberality, and of right which give nobility of character to a republic. In the interests of humanity, of civilization, and of progress, it is to be hoped that this evil influence may be soon averted.

The steamer Virginius was on the 26th day of September, 1870, duly registered at the port of New York as a part of the commercial marine of the United States. On the 4th of October, 1870, having received the certificate of her register in the usual legal form, she sailed from the port of New York and has not since been within the territorial jurisdiction of the United States. On the 31st day of October last, while sailing under the flag of the United States on the high seas, she was forcibly seized by the Spanish gunboat Tornado, and was carried into the port of Santiago de Cuba, where fifty-three of her passengers and crew were inhumanly, and, so far at least as relates to those who were citizens of the United States, without due process of law, put to death.

It is a well-established principle, asserted by the United States from the beginning of their national independence, recognized by Great Britain and other maritime powers, and stated by the Senate in a resolution passed unanimously on the 16th of June, 1858, that—American vessels on the high seas in time of peace, bearing the American flag, remain under the jurisdiction of the country to which they belong, and therefore any visitation, molestation, or detention of such vessel by force, or by the exhibition of force, on the part of a foreign power is in derogation of the sovereignty of the United States. In accordance with this principle, the restoration of the Virginius and the surrender of the survivors of her passengers and crew, and a due reparation to the flag, and the punishment of the authorities who had been guilty of the illegal acts of violence, were demanded. The Spanish Government has recognized the justice of the demand, and has arranged for the immediate delivery of the vessel, and for the surrender of the survivors of the passengers and crew, and for a salute to the flag, and for proceedings looking to the punishment of those who may be proved to have been guilty of illegal acts of violence toward citizens of the United States, and also toward indemnifying those who may be shown to be entitled to indemnity. A copy of a protocol of a conference between the Secretary of State and the Spanish minister, in which the terms of this arrangement were agreed to, is transmitted herewith.

The correspondence on this subject with the legation of the United States in Madrid was conducted in cipher and by cable, and needs the verification of the actual text of the correspondence. It has seemed to me to be due to the importance of the case not to submit this correspondence until the accurate text can be received by mail. It is expected shortly, and will be submitted when received.

In taking leave of this subject for the present I wish to renew the expression of my conviction that the existence of African slavery in Cuba is a principal cause of the lamentable condition of the island. I do not doubt that Congress shares with me the hope that it will soon be made to disappear, and that peace and prosperity may follow its abolition.

The embargoing of American estates in Cuba, cruelty to American citizens detected in no act of hostility to the Spanish Government, the murdering of prisoners taken with arms in their hands, and, finally, the capture upon the high seas of a vessel sailing under the United States flag and bearing a United States registry have culminated in an outburst of indignation that has seemed for a time to threaten war. Pending negotiations between the United States and the Government of Spain on the subject of this capture, I have authorized the Secretary of the Navy to put our Navy on a war footing, to the extent, at least, of the entire annual appropriation for that branch of the service, trusting to Congress and the public opinion of the American people to justify my action.

Assuming from the action of the last Congress in appointing a Committee on Privileges and Elections to prepare and report to this Congress a constitutional amendment to provide a better method of electing the President and Vice-President of the United States, and also from the necessity of such an amendment, that there will be submitted to the State legislatures for ratification such an improvement in our Constitution, I suggest two others for your consideration:

First. To authorize the Executive to approve of so much of any measure passing the two Houses of Congress as his judgment may dictate, without approving the whole, the disapproved portion or portions to be subjected to the same rules as now, to wit, to be referred back to the House in which the measure or measures originated, and, if passed by a two-thirds vote of the two Houses, then to become a law without the approval of the President. I would add to this a provision that there should be no legislation by Congress during the last twenty-four hours of its sitting, except upon vetoes, in order to give the Executive an opportunity to examine and approve or disapprove bills understandingly.

Second. To provide by amendment that when an extra session of Congress is convened by Executive proclamation legislation during the continuance of such extra session shall be confined to such subjects as the Executive may bring before it from time to time in writing.

The advantages to be gained by these two amendments are too obvious for me to comment upon them. One session in each year is provided for by the

Constitution, in which there are no restrictions as to the subjects of legislation by Congress. If more are required, it is always in the power of Congress, during their term of office, to provide for sessions at any time. The first of these amendments would protect the public against the many abuses and waste of public moneys which creep into appropriation bills and other important measures passing during the expiring hours of Congress, to which otherwise due consideration can not be given.

TREASURY DEPARTMENT.

The receipts of the Government from all sources for the last fiscal year were $333,738,204, and expenditures on all accounts $290,345,245, thus showing an excess of receipts over expenditures of $43,392,959. But it is not probable that this favorable exhibit will be shown for the present fiscal year. Indeed, it is very doubtful whether, except with great economy on the part of Congress in making appropriations and the same economy in administering the various Departments of Government, the revenues will not fall short of meeting actual expenses, including interest on the public debt.

I commend to Congress such economy, and point out two sources where It seems to me it might commence, to wit, in the appropriations for public buildings in the many cities where work has not yet been commenced; in the appropriations for river and harbor improvement in those localities where the improvements are of but little benefit to general commerce, and for fortifications.

There is a still more fruitful source of expenditure, which I will point out later in this message. I refer to the easy method of manufacturing claims for losses incurred in suppressing the late rebellion.

I would not be understood here as opposing the erection of good, substantial, and even ornamental buildings by the Government wherever such buildings are needed. In fact, I approve of the Government owning its own buildings in all sections of the country, and hope the day is not far distant when it will not only possess them, but will erect in the capital suitable residences for all persons who now receive commutation for quarters or rent at Government expense, and for the Cabinet, thus setting an example to the States which may induce them to erect buildings for their Senators. But I would have this work conducted at a time when the revenues of the country would abundantly justify it.

The revenues have materially fallen off for the first five months of the present fiscal year from what they were expected to produce, owing to the general panic now prevailing, which commenced about the middle of September last. The full effect of this disaster, if it should not prove a "blessing in disguise," is yet to be demonstrated. In either event it is your duty to heed the lesson and to provide by wise and well-considered legislation, as far as it lies in your power, against its recurrence, and to take advantage of all benefits that may have accrued.

My own judgment is that, however much individuals may have suffered, one long step has been taken toward specie payments; that we can never have permanent prosperity until a specie basis is reached: and that a specie basis can not be reached and maintained until our exports, exclusive of gold, pay for our imports, interest due abroad, and other specie obligations, or so nearly so as to leave an appreciable accumulation of the precious metals in the country from the products of our mines.

The development of the mines of precious metals during the past year and the prospective development of them for years to come are gratifying in their results. Could but one-half of the gold extracted from the mines be retained at home, our advance toward specie payments would be rapid.

To increase our exports sufficient currency is required to keep all the industries of the country employed. Without this national as well as individual bankruptcy must ensue. Undue inflation, on the other hand, while it might give temporary relief, would only lead to inflation of prices, the impossibility of competing in our own markets for the products of home skill and labor, and repeated renewals of present experiences. Elasticity to our circulating medium, therefore, and just enough of it to transact the legitimate business of the country and to keep all industries employed, is what is most to be desired. The exact medium is specie, the recognized medium of exchange the world over. That obtained, we shall have a currency of an exact degree of elasticity. If there be too much of it for the legitimate purposes of trade and commerce, it will flow out of the country. If too little, the reverse will result. To hold what we have and to appreciate our currency to that standard is the problem deserving of the most serious consideration of Congress.

The experience of the present panic has proven that the currency of the country, based, as it is, upon the credit of the country, is the best that has ever been devised. Usually in times of such trials currency has become worthless, or so much depreciated in value as to inflate the values of all the necessaries of life as compared with the currency. Everyone holding it has been anxious to dispose of it on any terms. Now we witness the reverse. Holders of currency hoard it as they did gold in former experiences of a like nature.

It is patent to the most casual observer that much more currency, or money, is required to transact the legitimate trade of the country during the fall and winter months, when the vast crops are being removed, than during the balance of the year. With our present system the amount in the country remains the same throughout the entire year, resulting in an accumulation of all the surplus capital of the country in a few centers when not employed in the moving of crops, tempted there by the offer of interest on call loans. Interest being paid, this surplus capital must earn this interest paid with a profit. Being subject to "call," it can not be loaned, only in part at best, to the merchant or manufacturer for a fixed term. Hence, no matter how much currency there might be in the country, it would be absorbed, prices keeping pace with the volume, and panics, stringency, and disasters would ever be recurring with the autumn. Elasticity in our monetary system, therefore, is the object to be attained first, and next to that, as far as possible, a prevention of the use of other people's money in stock and other species of speculation. To prevent the latter it seems to me that one great step would be taken by prohibiting the national banks from paying interest on deposits, by requiring them to hold their reserves in their own vaults, and by forcing them into resumption, though it would only be in legal-tender notes. For this purpose I would suggest the establishment of clearing houses for your consideration.

To secure the former many plans have been suggested, most, if not all, of which look to me more like inflation on the one hand, or compelling the Government, on the other, to pay interest, without corresponding benefits, upon the surplus funds of the country during the seasons when otherwise unemployed.

I submit for your consideration whether this difficulty might not be overcome by authorizing the Secretary of the Treasury to issue at any time to national banks of issue any amount of their own notes below a fixed percentage of their issue (say 40 per cent), upon the banks' depositing with the Treasurer of the United States an amount of Government bonds equal to the amount of notes demanded, the banks to forfeit to the Government, say, 4 per cent of the interest accruing on the bonds so pledged during the time they remain with the Treasurer as security for the increased circulation, the bonds so pledged to be redeemable by the banks at their pleasure, either in whole or in part, by returning their own bills for cancellation to an amount equal to the face of the bonds withdrawn. I would further suggest for your consideration the propriety of authorizing national banks to diminish their standing issue at pleasure, by returning for cancellation their own bills and withdrawing so many United States bonds as are pledged for the bills returned.

In view of the great actual contraction that has taken place in the currency and the comparative contraction continuously going on, due to the increase of population, increase of manufactories and all the industries, I do not believe there is too much of it now for the dullest period of the year. Indeed, if clearing houses should be established, thus forcing redemption, it is a question for your consideration whether banking should not be made free, retaining all the safeguards now required to secure bill holders. In any modification of the present laws regulating national banks, as a further step toward preparing for resumption of specie payments, I invite your attention to a consideration of the propriety of exacting from them the retention as a part of their reserve either the whole or a part of the gold interest accruing upon the bonds pledged as security for their issue. I have not reflected enough on the bearing this might have in producing a scarcity of coin with which to pay duties on imports to give it my positive recommendation. But your attention is invited to the subject.

During the last four years the currency has been contracted, directly, by the withdrawal of 3 per cent certificates, compound-interest notes, and "seven-thirty" bonds outstanding on the 4th of March, 1869, all of which took the place of legal-tenders in the bank reserves to the extent of $63,000,000.

During the same period there has been a much larger comparative contraction of the currency. The population of the country has largely increased. More than 25,000 miles of railroad have been built, requiring the active use of capital to operate them. Millions of acres of land have been opened to cultivation, requiring capital to move the products. Manufactories have multiplied beyond all precedent in the same period of time, requiring capital weekly for the payment of wages and for the purchase of material; and probably the largest of all comparative contraction arises from the organizing of free labor in the South. Now every laborer there receives his wages, and, for want of savings banks, the greater part of such wages is carried in the pocket or hoarded until required for use.

These suggestions are thrown out for your consideration, without any recommendation that they shall be adopted literally, but hoping that the best method may be arrived at to secure such an elasticity of the currency as will keep employed all the industries of the country and prevent such an inflation as will put off indefinitely the resumption of specie payments, an object so devoutly to be wished for by all, and by none more earnestly than the class of people most directly interested—those who "earn their bread by the sweat of their brow." The decisions of Congress on this subject will have the hearty support of the Executive.

In previous messages I have called attention to the decline in American shipbuilding and recommended such legislation as would secure to us our proportion of the carrying trade. Stimulated by high rates and abundance of freight, the progress for the last year in shipbuilding has been very satisfactory. There has been an increase of about 3 per cent in the amount transported in American vessels over the amount of last year. With the reduced cost of material which has taken place, it may reasonably be hoped that this progress will be maintained, and even increased. However, as we pay about $80,000,000 per annum to foreign vessels for the transportation to a market of our surplus products, thus increasing the balance of trade against us to this amount, the subject is one worthy of your serious consideration.

"Cheap transportation" is a subject that has attracted the attention of both producers and consumers for the past few years, and has contributed to, if it has not been the direct cause of, the recent panic and stringency.

As Congress, at its last session, appointed a special committee to investigate this whole subject during the vacation and report at this session, I have nothing to recommend until their report is read.

There is one work, however, of a national character, in which the greater portion of the East and the West, the North and the South, are equally interested, to which I will invite your attention.

The State of New York has a canal connecting Lake Erie with tide water on the Hudson River. The State of Illinois has a similar work connecting Lake Michigan with navigable water on the Illinois River, thus making water communication inland between the East and the West and South. These great artificial water courses are the property of the States through which they pass, and pay toll to those States. Would it not be wise statesmanship to pledge these States that if they will open these canals for the passage of large vessels the General Government will look after and keep in navigable condition the great public highways with which they connect, to wit, the Overslaugh on the Hudson, the St. Clair Flats, and the Illinois and Mississippi rivers? This would be a national work; one of great value to the producers of the West and South in giving them cheap transportation for their produce to the seaboard and a market, and to the consumers in the East in giving them cheaper food, particularly of those articles of food which do not find a foreign market, and the prices of which, therefore, are not regulated by foreign demands. The advantages of such a work are too obvious for argument. I submit the subject to you, therefore, without further comment.

In attempting to regain our lost commerce and carrying trade I have heretofore called attention to the States south of us offering a field where much might be accomplished. To further this object I suggest that a small appropriation be made, accompanied with authority for the Secretary of the Navy to fit out a naval vessel to ascend the Amazon River to the mouth of the Madeira; thence to explore that river and its tributaries into Bolivia, and to report to Congress at its next session, or as soon as practicable, the accessibility of the country by water, its resources, and the population so reached. Such an exploration would cost but little; it can do no harm, and may result in establishing a trade of value to both nations.

In further connection with the Treasury Department I would recommend a revision and codification of the tariff laws and the opening of more mints for coining money, with authority to coin for such nations as may apply.

WAR DEPARTMENT.

The attention of Congress is invited to the recommendations contained in the report of the Secretary of War herewith accompanying.

The apparent great cost of supporting the Army is fully explained by this report, and I hope will receive your attention.

While inviting your general attention to all the recommendations made by the Secretary of War, there are two which I would especially invite you to consider: First, the importance of preparing for war in time of peace by providing proper armament for our seacoast defenses. Proper armament is of vastly more importance than fortifications. The latter can be supplied very speedily for temporary purposes when needed; the former can not. The second is the necessity of reopening promotion in the staff corps of the Army. Particularly is this necessity felt in the Medical, Pay, and Ordnance departments.

At this time it is necessary to employ "contract surgeons" to supply the necessary medical attendance required by the Army.

With the present force of the Pay Department it is now difficult to make the payments to troops provided for by law. Long delays in payments are productive of desertions and other demoralization, and the law prohibits the payment of troops by other than regular army paymasters.

There are now sixteen vacancies in the Ordnance Department, thus leaving that branch of the service without sufficient officers to conduct the business of the different arsenals on a large scale if ever required.

NAVY DEPARTMENT.

During the past year our Navy has been depleted by the sale of some vessels no longer fit for naval service and by the condemnation of others not yet disposed of. This, however, has been more than compensated for by the repair of six of the old wooden ships and by the building of eight new sloops of war, authorized by the last Congress. The building of these latter has occurred at a doubly fortunate time. They are about being completed at a time when they may possibly be much needed, and the work upon them has not only given direct employment to thousands of men, but has no doubt been the means of keeping open establishments for other work at a time of great financial distress.

Since the commencement of the last month, however, the distressing occurrences which have taken place in the waters of the Caribbean Sea, almost on our very seaboard, while they illustrate most forcibly the necessity always existing that a nation situated like ours should maintain in a state of possible efficiency a navy adequate to its responsibilities, has at the same time demanded that all the effective force we really have shall be put in immediate readiness for warlike service. This has been and is being done promptly and effectively, and I am assured that all the available ships and every authorized man of the American Navy will be ready for whatever action is required for the safety of our citizens or the maintenance of our honor. This, of course, will require the expenditure in a short time of some of the appropriations which were calculated to extend through the fiscal year, but Congress will, I doubt not, understand and appreciate the emergency, and will provide adequately not only for the present preparation, but for the future maintenance of our naval force. The Secretary of the Navy has during the past year been quietly putting some of our most effective monitors in condition for service, and thus the exigency finds us in a much better condition for work than we could possibly have been without his action.

POST-OFFICE DEPARTMENT.

A complete exhibit is presented in the accompanying report of the postmaster-General of the operations of the Post-Office Department during the year. The ordinary postal revenues for the fiscal year ended June 30, 1873, amounted to $22,996,741.57, and the expenditures of all kinds to $29,084,945.67. The increase of revenues over 1872 was $1,081,315.20, and the increase of expenditures $2,426,753.36.

Independent of the payments made from special appropriations for mail steamship lines, the amount drawn from the General Treasury to meet deficiencies was $5,265,475. The constant and rapid extension of our postal service, particularly upon railways, and the improved facilities for the collection, transmission, distribution, and delivery of the mails which are constantly being provided account for the increased expenditures of this popular branch of the public service.

The total number of post-offices in operation on June 30, 1873, was 33,244, a net increase of 1,381 over the number reported the preceding year. The number of Presidential offices was 1,363, an increase of 163 during the year. The total length of railroad mail routes at the close of the year was 63,457 miles, an increase of 5,546 miles over the year 1872. Fifty-nine railway post-office lines were in operation June 30, 1873, extending over 14,866 miles of railroad routes and performing an aggregate service of 34,925 miles daily.

The number of letters exchanged with foreign countries was 27,459,185, an increase of 3,096,685 over the previous year, and the postage thereon amounted to $2,021,310.86. The total weight of correspondence exchanged in the mails with European countries exceeded 912 tons, an increase of 92 tons over the previous year. The total cost of the United States ocean steamship service, including $725,000 paid from special appropriations to subsidized lines of mail steamers, was $1,047,271.35.

New or additional postal conventions have been concluded with Sweden, Norway, Belgium, Germany, Canada, Newfoundland, and Japan, reducing postage rates on correspondence exchanged with those countries; and further efforts have been made to conclude a satisfactory postal convention with France, but without success.

I invite the favorable consideration of Congress to the suggestions and recommendations of the Postmaster-General for an extension of the free-delivery system in all cities having a population of not less than 10,000; for the prepayment of postage on newspapers and other printed matter of the second class; for a uniform postage and limit of weight on miscellaneous matter; for adjusting the compensation of all postmasters not appointed by the President, by the old method of commissions on the actual receipts of the office, instead of the present mode of fixing the salary in advance upon special returns; and especially do I urge favorable action by Congress on the important recommendations of the Postmaster-General for the establishment of United States postal savings depositories.

Your attention is also again called to a consideration of the question of postal telegraphs and the arguments adduced in support thereof, in the hope that you may take such action in connection therewith as in your judgment will most contribute to the best interests of the country.

DEPARTMENT OF JUSTICE.

Affairs in Utah require your early and special attention. The Supreme Court of the United States, in the case of Clinton vs. Englebrecht, decided that the United States marshal of that Territory could not lawfully summon jurors for the district courts; and those courts hold that the Territorial marshal can not lawfully perform that duty, because he is elected by the legislative assembly, and not appointed as provided for in the act organizing the Territory. All proceedings at law are practically abolished by these decisions, and there have been but few or no jury trials in the district courts of that Territory since the last session of Congress. Property is left without protection by the courts, and crimes go unpunished. To prevent anarchy there it is absolutely necessary that Congress provide the courts with some mode of obtaining jurors, and I recommend legislation to that end, and also that the probate courts of the Territory, now assuming to issue writs of injunction and habeas corpus and to try criminal cases and questions as to land titles, be denied all jurisdiction not possessed ordinarily by courts of that description.

I have become impressed with the belief that the act approved March 2, 1867, entitled "An act to establish a uniform system of bankruptcy throughout the United States," is productive of more evil than good at this time. Many considerations might be urged for its total repeal, but, if this is not considered advisable, I think it will not be seriously questioned that those portions of said act providing for what is called involuntary bankruptcy operate to increase the financial embarrassments of the country. Careful and prudent men very often become involved in debt in the transaction of their business, and though they may possess ample property, if it could be made available for that purpose, to meet all their liabilities, yet, on account of the extraordinary scarcity of money, they may be unable to meet all their pecuniary obligations as they become due, in consequence of which they are liable to be prostrated in their business by proceedings in bankruptcy at the instance of unrelenting creditors. People are now so easily alarmed as to monetary matters that the mere filing of a petition in bankruptcy by an unfriendly creditor will necessarily embarrass, and oftentimes accomplish the financial ruin, of a responsible business man. Those who otherwise might make lawful and just arrangements to relieve themselves from difficulties produced by the present stringency in money are prevented by their constant exposure to attack and disappointment by proceedings against them in bankruptcy, and, besides, the law is made use of in many cases by obdurate creditors to frighten or force debtors into a compliance with their wishes and into acts of injustice to other creditors and to themselves. I recommend that so much of said act as provides for involuntary bankruptcy on account of the suspension of payment be repealed.

Your careful attention is invited to the subject of claims against the Government and to the facilities afforded by existing laws for their prosecution. Each of the Departments of State, Treasury, and War has demands for many millions of dollars upon its files, and they are rapidly accumulating. To these may be added those now pending before Congress, the Court of Claims, and the Southern Claims Commission, making in the aggregate an immense sum. Most of these grow out of the rebellion, and are intended to indemnify persons on both sides for their losses during the war; and not a few of them are fabricated and supported by false testimony. Projects are on foot, it is believed, to induce Congress to provide for new classes of claims, and to revive old ones through the repeal or modification of the statute of limitations, by which they are now barred. I presume these schemes, if proposed, will be received with little favor by Congress, and I recommend that persons having claims against the United States cognizable by any tribunal or Department thereof be required to present them at an early day, and that legislation be directed as far as practicable to the defeat of unfounded and unjust demands upon the Government; and I would suggest, as a means of preventing fraud, that witnesses be called upon to appear in person to testify before those tribunals having said claims before them for adjudication. Probably the largest saving to the National Treasury can be secured by timely legislation on these subjects of any of the economic measures that will be proposed.

You will be advised of the operations of the Department of Justice by the report of the Attorney-General, and I invite your attention to the amendments of existing laws suggested by him, with the view of reducing the expenses of that Department.

DEPARTMENT OF THE INTERIOR.

The policy inaugurated toward the Indians at the beginning of the last Administration has been steadily pursued, and, I believe, with beneficial results. It will be continued with only such modifications as time and experience may demonstrate as necessary.

With the encroachment of civilization upon the Indian reservations and hunting grounds, disturbances have taken place between the Indians and whites during the past year, and probably will continue to do so until each race appreciates that the other has rights which must be respected.

The policy has been to collect the Indians as rapidly as possible on reservations, and as far as practicable within what is known as the Indian Territory, and to teach them the arts of civilization and self-support. Where found off their reservations, and endangering the peace and safety of the whites, they have been punished, and will continue to be for like offenses.

The Indian Territory south of Kansas and west of Arkansas is sufficient in area and agricultural resources to support all the Indians east of the Rocky Mountains. In time, no doubt, all of them, except a few who may elect to make their homes among white people, will be collected there. As a preparatory step for this consummation, I am now satisfied that a Territorial form of government should be given them, which will secure the treaty rights of the original settlers and protect their homesteads from alienation for a period of twenty years.

The operations of the Patent Office are growing to such a magnitude and the accumulation of material is becoming so great that the necessity of more room is becoming more obvious day by day. I respectfully invite your attention to the reports of the Secretary of the Interior and Commissioner of Patents on this subject.

The business of the General Land Office exhibits a material increase in all its branches during the last fiscal year. During that time there were disposed of out of the public lands 13,030,606 acres, being an amount greater by 1,165,631 acres than was disposed of during the preceding year. Of the amount disposed of, 1,626,266 acres were sold for cash, 214,940 acres were located with military land warrants, 3,793,612 acres were taken for homesteads, 653,446 acres were located with agricultural-college scrip, 6,083,536 acres were certified by railroads, 76,576 acres were granted to wagon roads, 238,548 acres were approved to States as swamp lands, 138,681 acres were certified for agricultural colleges, common schools, universities, and seminaries, 190,775 acres were approved to States for internal improvements, and 14,222 acres were located with Indian scrip. The cash receipts during the same time were $3,408,515.50, being $190,415.50 in excess of the receipts of the previous year. During the year 30,488,132 acres of public land were surveyed, an increase over the amount surveyed the previous year of 1,037,193 acres, and, added to the area previously surveyed, aggregates 616,554,895 acres which have been surveyed, leaving 1,218,443,505 acres of the public land still unsurveyed.

The increased and steadily increasing facilities for reaching our unoccupied public domain and for the transportation of surplus products enlarge the available field for desirable homestead locations, thus stimulating settlement and extending year by year in a gradually increasing ratio the area of occupation and cultivation.

The expressed desire of the representatives of a large colony of citizens of Russia to emigrate to this country, as is understood, with the consent of their Government, if certain concessions can be made to enable them to settle in a compact colony, is of great interest, as going to show the light in which our institutions are regarded by an industrious, intelligent, and wealthy people, desirous of enjoying civil and religious liberty; and the acquisition of so large an immigration of citizens of a superior class would without doubt be of substantial benefit to the country. I invite attention to the suggestion of the Secretary of the Interior in this behalf.

There was paid during the last fiscal year for pensions, including the expense of disbursement, $29,185,289.62, being an amount less by $984,050.98 than was expended for the same purpose the preceding year. Although this statement of expenditures would indicate a material reduction in amount compared with the preceding year, it is believed that the changes in the pension laws at the last session of Congress will absorb that amount the current year. At the close of the last fiscal year there were on the pension rolls 99,804 invalid military pensioners and 112,088 widows, orphans, and dependent relatives of deceased soldiers, making a total of that class of 211,892; 18,266 survivors of the War of 1812 and 5,058 widows of soldiers of that war pensioned under the act of Congress of February 14, 1871, making a total of that class of 23,319; 1,480 invalid navy pensioners and 1,770 widows, orphans, and dependent relatives of deceased officers, sailors, and marines of the Navy, making a total of navy pensioners of 3,200, and a grand total of pensioners of 311 classes of 238,411, showing a net increase during the last fiscal year of 6,182. During the last year the names of 16,405 pensioners were added to the rolls, and 10,223 names were dropped therefrom for various causes.

The system adopted for the detection of frauds against the Government in the matter of pensions has been productive of satisfactory results, but legislation is needed to provide, if possible, against the perpetration of such frauds in future.

The evidently increasing interest in the cause of education is a most encouraging feature in the general progress and prosperity of the country, and the Bureau of Education is earnest in its efforts to give proper direction to the new appliances and increased facilities which are being offered to aid the educators of the country in their great work.

The Ninth Census has been completed, the report thereof published and distributed, and the working force of the Bureau disbanded. The Secretary of the Interior renews his recommendation for a census to be taken in 1875, to which subject the attention of Congress is invited. The original suggestion in that behalf has met with the general approval of the country;

and even if it be not deemed advisable at present to provide for a regular quinquennial census, a census taken in 1875, the report of which could be completed and published before the one hundredth anniversary of our national independence, would be especially interesting and valuable, as showing the progress of the country during the first century of our national existence. It is believed, however, that a regular census every five years would be of substantial benefit to the country, inasmuch as our growth hitherto has been so rapid that the results of the decennial census are necessarily unreliable as a basis of estimates for the latter years of a decennial period.

DISTRICT OF COLUMBIA.

Under the very efficient management of the governor and the board of public works of this District the city of Washington is rapidly assuming the appearance of a capital of which the nation may well be proud. From being a most unsightly place three years ago, disagreeable to pass through in summer in consequence of the dust arising from unpaved streets, and almost impassable in the winter from the mud, it is now one of the most sightly cities in the country, and can boast of being the best paved.

The work has been done systematically, the plans, grades, location of sewers, water and gas mains being determined upon before the work was commenced, thus securing permanency when completed. I question whether so much has ever been accomplished before in any American city for the same expenditures. The Government having large reservations in the city, and the nation at large having an interest in their capital, I recommend a liberal policy toward the District of Columbia, and that the Government should bear its just share of the expense of these improvements. Every citizen visiting the capital feels a pride in its growing beauty, and that he too is part owner in the investments made here.

I would suggest to Congress the propriety of promoting the establishment in this District of an institution of learning, or university of the highest class, by the donation of lands. There is no place better suited for such an institution than the national capital. There is no other place in which every citizen is so directly interested.

CIVIL-SERVICE REFORM.

In three successive messages to Congress I have called attention to the subject of "civil-service reform."

Action has been taken so far as to authorize the appointment of a board to devise rules governing methods of making appointments and promotions, but there never has been any action making these rules, or any rules, binding, or even entitled to observance, where persons desire the appointment of a friend or the removal of an official who may be disagreeable to them.

To have any rules effective they must have the acquiescence of Congress as well as of the Executive. I commend, therefore, the subject to your attention, and suggest that a special committee of Congress might confer with the Civil-Service Board during the present session for the purpose of devising such rules as can be maintained, and which will secure the services of honest and capable officials, and which will also protect them in a degree of independence while in office.

Proper rules will protect Congress, as well as the Executive, from much needless persecution, and will prove of great value to the public at large.

I would recommend for your favorable consideration the passage of an enabling act for the admission of Colorado as a State in the Union. It possesses all the elements of a prosperous State, agricultural and mineral, and, I believe, has a population now to justify such admission. In connection with this I would also recommend the encouragement of a canal for purposes of irrigation from the eastern slope of the Rocky Mountains to the Missouri River. As a rule I am opposed to further donations of public lands for internal improvements owned and controlled by private corporations, but in this instance I would make an exception. Between the Missouri River and the Rocky Mountains there is an arid belt of public land from 300 to 500 miles in width, perfectly valueless for the occupation of man, for the want of sufficient rain to secure the growth of any product. An irrigating canal would make productive a belt as wide as the supply of water could be made to spread over across this entire country, and would secure a cordon of settlements connecting the present population of the mountain and mining regions with that of the older States. All the land reclaimed would be clear gain. If alternate sections are retained by the Government, I would suggest that the retained sections be thrown open to entry under the homestead laws, or sold to actual settlers for a very low price.

I renew my previous recommendation to Congress for general amnesty. The number engaged in the late rebellion yet laboring under disabilities is very small, but enough to keep up a constant irritation. No possible danger can accrue to the Government by restoring them to eligibility to hold office. I suggest for your consideration the enactment of a law to better secure the civil rights which freedom should secure, but has not effectually secured, to the enfranchised slave.

U. S. GRANT

December 7, 1874
To the Senate and House of Representatives:

Since the convening of Congress one year ago the nation has undergone a prostration in business and industries such as has not been witnessed with us for many years. Speculation as to the causes for this prostration might be indulged in without profit, because as many theories would be advanced as there would be independent writers—those who expressed their own views without borrowing—upon the subject. Without indulging in theories as to the cause of this prostration, therefore, I will call your attention only to the fact, and to some plain questions as to which it would seem there should be no disagreement.

During this prostration two essential elements of prosperity have been most abundant—labor and capital. Both have been largely unemployed. Where security has been undoubted, capital has been attainable at very moderate rates. Where labor has been wanted, it has been found in abundance, at cheap rates compared with what—of necessaries and comforts of life— could be purchased with the wages demanded. Two great elements of prosperity, therefore, have not been denied us. A third might be added: Our soil and climate are unequaled, within the limits of any contiguous territory under one nationality, for its variety of products to feed and clothe a people and in the amount of surplus to spare to feed less favored peoples. Therefore, with these facts in view, it seems to me that wise statesmanship, at this session of Congress, would dictate legislation ignoring the past; directing in proper channels these great elements of prosperity to any people. Debt, debt abroad, is the only element that can, with always a sound currency, enter into our affairs to cause any continued depression in the industries and prosperity of our people.

A great conflict for national existence made necessary, for temporary purposes, the raising of large sums of money from whatever source attainable. It made it necessary, in the wisdom of Congress—and I do not doubt their wisdom in the premises, regarding the necessity of the times— to devise a system of national currency which it proved to be impossible to keep on a par with the recognized currency of the civilized world. This begot a spirit of speculation involving an extravagance and luxury not required for the happiness or prosperity of a people, and involving, both directly and indirectly, foreign indebtedness. The currency, being of fluctuating value, and therefore unsafe to hold for legitimate transactions requiring money, became a subject of speculation within itself. These two causes, however, have involved us in a foreign indebtedness, contracted in good faith by borrower and lender, which should be paid in coin, and according to the bond agreed upon when the debt was contracted—gold or its equivalent. The good faith of the Government can not be violated toward creditors without national disgrace. But our commerce should be encouraged; American shipbuilding and carrying capacity increased; foreign markets sought for products of the soil and manufactories, to the end that we may be able to pay these debts. Where a new market can be created for the sale of our products, either of the soil, the mine, or the manufactory, a new means is discovered of utilizing our idle capital and labor to the advantage of the whole people. But, in my judgment, the first step toward accomplishing this object is to secure a currency of fixed, stable value; a currency good wherever civilization reigns; one which, if it becomes superabundant with one people, will find a market with some other; a currency which has as its basis the labor necessary to produce it, which will give to it its value. Gold and silver are now the recognized medium of exchange the civilized world over, and to this we should return with the least practicable delay. In view of the pledges of the American Congress when our present legal-tender system was adopted, and debt contracted, there should be no delay—certainly no unnecessary delay—in fixing by legislation a method by which we will return to specie. To the accomplishment of this end I invite your special attention. I believe firmly that there can be no prosperous and permanent revival of business and industries until a policy is adopted—with legislation to carry it out—looking to a return to a specie basis. It is easy to conceive that the debtor and speculative classes may think it of value to them to make so-called money abundant until they can throw a portion of their burdens upon others. But even these, I believe, would be disappointed in the result if a course should be pursued which will keep in doubt the value of the legal-tender medium of exchange. A revival of productive industry is needed by all classes; by none more than the holders of property, of whatever sort, with debts to liquidate from realization upon its sale. But admitting that these two classes of citizens are to be benefited by expansion, would it be honest to give it? Would not the general loss be too great to justify such relief? Would it not be just as honest and prudent to authorize each debtor to issue his own legal-tenders to the extent of his liabilities? Than to do this, would it not be safer, for fear of overissues by unscrupulous creditors, to say that all debt obligations are obliterated in the United States, and now we commence anew, each possessing all he has at the time free from incumbrance? These propositions are too absurd to be entertained for a moment by thinking or honest people. Yet every delay in preparation for final resumption partakes of this dishonesty, and is only less in degree as the hope is held out that a convenient season will at last arrive for the good work of redeeming our pledges to commence. It will never come, in my opinion, except by positive action by Congress, or by national disasters which will destroy, for a time at least, the credit of the individual and the State at large. A sound currency might be reached by total bankruptcy and discredit of the integrity of the nation and of individuals. I believe it is in the power of Congress at this session to devise such legislation as will renew confidence, revive all the industries, start us on a career of prosperity to last for many years and to save the credit of the nation and of the people. Steps toward the return to a specie basis are the great requisites to this devoutly to be sought for end. There are others which I may touch upon hereafter.

A nation dealing in a currency below that of specie in value labors under two great disadvantages: First, having no use for the world's acknowledged medium of exchange, gold and silver, these are driven out of the country because there is no need for their use; second, the medium of exchange in use being of a fluctuating value—for, after all, it is only worth just what it will purchase of gold and silver, metals having an intrinsic value just in proportion to the honest labor it takes to produce them—a larger margin must be allowed for profit by the manufacturer and producer. It is months from the date of production to the date of realization. Interest upon capital must be charged, and risk of fluctuation in the value of that which is to be received in payment added. Hence high prices, acting as a protection to the foreign producer, who receives nothing in exchange for the products of his skill and labor except a currency good, at a stable value, the world over It seems to me that nothing is clearer than that the greater part of the burden of existing prostration, for the want of a sound financial system, falls upon the working man, who must after all produce the wealth, and the salaried man, who superintends and conducts business. The burden falls upon them in two ways—by the deprivation of employment and by the decreased purchasing power of their salaries. It is the duty of Congress to devise the method of correcting the evils which are acknowledged to exist, and not mine. But I will venture to suggest two or three things which seem to me as absolutely necessary to a return to specie payments, the first great requisite in a return to prosperity. The legal-tender clause to the law authorizing the issue of currency by the National Government should be repealed, to take effect as to all contracts entered into after a day fixed in the repealing act— not to apply, however, to payments of salaries by Government, or for other expenditures now provided by law to be paid in currency, in the interval pending between repeal and final resumption. Provision should be made by which the Secretary of the Treasury can obtain gold as it may become necessary from time to time from the date when specie redemption commences. To this might and should be added a revenue sufficiently in excess of expenses to insure an accumulation of gold in the Treasury to sustain permanent redemption.

I commend this subject to your careful consideration, believing that a favorable solution is attainable, and if reached by this Congress that the present and future generations will ever gratefully remember it as their deliverer from a thraldom of evil and disgrace.

With resumption, free banking may be authorized with safety, giving the same full protection to bill holders which they have under existing laws. Indeed, I would regard free banking as essential. It would give proper elasticity to the currency. As more currency should be required for the transaction of legitimate business, new banks would be started, and in turn banks would wind up their business when it was found that there was a superabundance of currency. The experience and judgment of the people can best decide just how much currency is required for the transaction of the business of the country. It is unsafe to leave the settlement of this question to Congress, the Secretary of the Treasury, or the Executive. Congress should make the regulation under which banks may exist, but should not make banking a monopoly by limiting the amount of redeemable paper currency that shall be authorized. Such importance do I attach to this subject, and so earnestly do I commend it to your attention, that I give it prominence by introducing it at the beginning of this message.

During the past year nothing has occurred to disturb the general friendly and cordial relations of the United States with other powers.

The correspondence submitted herewith between this Government and its diplomatic representatives, as also with the representatives of other countries, shows a satisfactory condition of all questions between the United States and the most of those countries, and with few exceptions, to which reference is hereafter made, the absence of any points of difference to be adjusted.

The notice directed by the resolution of Congress of June 17, 1874, to be given to terminate the convention of July 17, 1858, between the United States and Belgium has been given, and the treaty will accordingly terminate on the 1st day of July, 1875. This convention secured to certain Belgian vessels entering the ports of the United States exceptional privileges which are not accorded to our own vessels. Other features of the convention have proved satisfactory, and have tended to the cultivation of mutually beneficial commercial intercourse and friendly relations between the two countries. I hope that negotiations which have been invited will result in the celebration of another treaty which may tend to the interests of both countries.

Our relations with China continue to be friendly. During the past year the fear of hostilities between China and Japan, growing out of the landing of an armed force upon the island of Formosa by the latter, has occasioned uneasiness. It is earnestly hoped, however, that the difficulties arising from this cause will be adjusted, and that the advance of civilization in these Empires may not be retarded by a state of war. In consequence of the part taken by certain citizens of the United States in this expedition, our representatives in those countries have been instructed to impress upon the Governments of China and Japan the firm intention of this country to maintain strict neutrality in the event of hostilities, and to carefully prevent any infraction of law on the part of our citizens.

In connection with this subject I call the attention of Congress to a generally conceded fact—that the great proportion of the Chinese immigrants who come to our shores do not come voluntarily, to make their homes with us and their labor productive of general prosperity, but come under contracts with headmen, who own them almost absolutely. In a worse form does this apply to Chinese women. Hardly a perceptible percentage of them perform any honorable labor, but they are brought for shameful purposes, to the disgrace of the communities where settled and to the great demoralization of the youth of those localities. If this evil practice can be legislated against, it will be my pleasure as well as duty to enforce any regulation to secure so desirable an end.

It is hoped that negotiations between the Government of Japan and the treaty powers, looking to the further opening of the Empire and to the removal of various restrictions upon trade and travel, may soon produce the results desired, which can not fail to inure to the benefit of all the parties. Having on previous occasions submitted to the consideration of Congress the propriety of the release of the Japanese Government from the further payment of the indemnity under the convention of October 22, 1864, and as no action had been taken thereon, it became my duty to regard the obligations of the convention as in force; and as the other powers interested had received their portion of the indemnity in full, the minister of the United States in Japan has, in behalf of this Government, received the remainder of the amount due to the United States under the convention of Simonosaki. I submit the propriety of applying the income of a part, if not of the whole, of this fund to the education in the Japanese language of a number of young men to be under obligations to serve the Government for a specified time as interpreters at the legation and the consulates in Japan. A limited number of Japanese youths might at the same time be educated in our own vernacular, and mutual benefits would result to both Governments. The importance of having our own citizens, competent and familiar with the language of Japan, to act as interpreters and in other capacities connected with the legation and the consulates in that country can not readily be overestimated.

The amount awarded to the Government of Great Britain by the mixed commission organized under the provisions of the treaty of Washington in settlement of the claims of British subjects arising from acts committed between April 13, 1861, and April 9, 1865, became payable, under the terms of the treaty, within the past year, and was paid upon the 21st day of September, 1874. In this connection I renew my recommendation, made at the opening of the last session of Congress, that a special court be created to hear and determine all claims of aliens against the United States arising from acts committed against their persons or property during the insurrection. It appears equitable that opportunity should be offered to citizens of other states to present their claims, as well as to those British subjects whose claims were not admissible under the late commission, to the early decision of some competent tribunal. To this end I recommend the necessary legislation to organize a court to dispose of all claims of aliens of the nature referred to in an equitable and satisfactory manner, and to relieve Congress and the Departments from the consideration of these questions.

The legislation necessary to extend to the colony of Newfoundland certain articles of the treaty of Washington of the 8th day of May, 1871, having been had, a protocol to that effect was signed in behalf of the United States and of Great Britain on the 28th day of May last, and was duly proclaimed on the following day. A copy of the proclamation is submitted herewith.

A copy of the report of the commissioner appointed under the act of March 19, 1872, for surveying and marking the boundary between the United States and the British possessions from the Lake of the Woods to the summit of the Rocky Mountains is herewith transmitted. I am happy to announce that the field work of the commission has been completed, and the entire line from the northwest corner of the Lake of the Woods to the summit of the Rocky Mountains has been run and marked upon the surface of the earth. It is believed that the amount remaining unexpended of the appropriation made at the last session of Congress will be sufficient to complete the office work. I recommend that the authority of Congress be given to the use of the unexpended balance of the appropriation in the completion of the work of the commission in making its report and preparing the necessary maps.

The court known as the Court of Commissioners of Alabama Claims, created by an act of Congress of the last session, has organized and commenced its work, and it is to be hoped that the claims admissible under the provisions of the act may be speedily ascertained and paid.

It has been deemed advisable to exercise the discretion conferred upon the Executive at the last session by accepting the conditions required by the Government of Turkey for the privilege of allowing citizens of the United States to hold real estate in the former country, and by assenting to a certain change in the jurisdiction of courts in the latter. A copy of the proclamation upon these subjects is herewith communicated.

There has been no material change in our relations with the independent States of this hemisphere which were formerly under the dominion of Spain. Marauding on the frontiers between Mexico and Texas still frequently takes place, despite the vigilance of the civil and military authorities in that quarter. The difficulty of checking such trespasses along the course of a river of such length as the Rio Grande, and so often fordable, is obvious. It is hoped that the efforts of this Government will be seconded by those of Mexico to the effectual suppression of these acts of wrong.

From a report upon the condition of the business before the American and Mexican Joint Claims Commission, made by the agent on the part of the United States, and dated October 28, 1874, it appears that of the 1,017 claims filed on the part of citizens of the United States, 483 had been finally decided and 75 were in the hands of the umpire, leaving 462 to be disposed of; and of the 998 claims filed against the United States, 726 had been finally decided, I was before the umpire, and 271 remained to be disposed of. Since the date of such report other claims have been disposed of, reducing somewhat the number still pending; and others have been passed upon by the arbitrators. It has become apparent, in view of these figures and of the fact that the work devolving on the umpire is particularly laborious, that the commission will be unable to dispose of the entire number of claims pending prior to the 1st day of February, 1875—the date fixed for its expiration. Negotiations are pending looking to the securing of the results of the decisions which have been reached and to a further extension of the commission for a limited time, which it is confidently hoped will suffice to bring all the business now before it to a final close.

The strife in the Argentine Republic is to be deplored, both on account of the parties thereto and from the probable effects on the interests of those engaged in the trade to that quarter, of whom the United States are among the principal. As yet, so far as I am aware, there has been no violation of our neutrality rights, which, as well as our duties in that respect, it shall be my endeavor to maintain and observe.

It is with regret I announce that no further payment has been received from the Government of Venezuela on account of awards in favor of citizens of the United States. Hopes have been entertained that if that Republic could escape both foreign and civil war for a few years its great natural resources would enable it to honor its obligations. Though it is now understood to be at peace with other countries, a serious insurrection is reported to be in progress in an important region of that Republic. This may be taken advantage of as another reason to delay the payment of the dues of our citizens.

The deplorable strife in Cuba continues without any marked change in the relative advantages of the contending forces. The insurrection continues, but Spain has gained no superiority. Six years of strife give to the insurrection a significance which can not be denied. Its duration and the tenacity of its adherence, together with the absence of manifested power of suppression on the part of Spain, can not be controverted, and may make some positive steps on the part of other powers a matter of self-necessity. I had confidently hoped at this time to be able to announce the arrangement of some of the important questions between this Government and that of Spain, but the negotiations have been protracted. The unhappy intestine dissensions of Spain command our profound sympathy, and must be accepted as perhaps a cause of some delay. An early settlement, in part at least, of the questions between the Governments is hoped. In the meantime, awaiting the results of immediately pending negotiations, I defer a further and fuller communication on the subject of the relations of this country and Spain.

I have again to call the attention of Congress to the unsatisfactory condition of the existing laws with reference to expatriation and the election of nationality. Formerly, amid conflicting opinions and decisions, it was difficult to exactly determine how far the doctrine of perpetual allegiance was applicable to citizens of the United States. Congress by the act of the 27th of July, 1868, asserted the abstract right of expatriation as a fundamental principle of this Government. Notwithstanding such assertion and the necessity of frequent application of the principle, no legislation has been had defining what acts or formalities shall work expatriation or when a citizen shall be deemed to have renounced or to have lost his citizenship. The importance of such definition is obvious. The representatives of the United States in foreign countries are continually called upon to lend their aid and the protection of the United States to persons concerning the good faith or the reality of whose citizenship there is at least great question. In some cases the provisions of the treaties furnish some guide; in others it seems left to the person claiming the benefits of citizenship, while living in a foreign country, contributing in no manner to the performance of the duties of a citizen of the United States, and without intention at any time to return and undertake those duties, to use the claims to citizenship of the United States simply as a shield from the performance of the obligations of a citizen elsewhere.

The status of children born of American parents residing in a foreign country, of American women who have married aliens, of American citizens residing abroad where such question is not regulated by treaty, are all sources of frequent difficulty and discussion. Legislation on these and similar questions, and particularly defining when and under what circumstances expatriation can be accomplished or is to be presumed, is especially needed. In this connection I earnestly call the attention of Congress to the difficulties arising from fraudulent naturalization. The United States wisely, freely, and liberally offers its citizenship to all who may come in good faith to reside within its limits on their complying with certain prescribed reasonable and simple formalities and conditions. Among the highest duties of the Government is that to afford firm, sufficient, and equal protection to all its citizens, whether native born or naturalized. Care should be taken that a right carrying with it such support from the Government should not be fraudulently obtained, and should be bestowed only upon full proof of a compliance with the law; and yet frequent instances are brought to the attention of the Government of illegal and fraudulent naturalization and of the unauthorized use of certificates thus improperly obtained. In some cases the fraudulent character of the naturalization has appeared upon the face of the certificate itself; in others examination discloses that the holder had not complied with the law, and in others certificates have been obtained where the persons holding them not only were not entitled to be naturalized, but had not even been within the United States at the time of the pretended naturalization. Instances of each of these classes of fraud are discovered at our legations, where the certificates of naturalization are presented either for the purpose of obtaining passports or in demanding the protection of the legation. When the fraud is apparent on the face of such certificates, they are taken up by the representatives of the Government and forwarded to the Department of State. But even then the record of the court in which the fraudulent naturalization occurred remains, and duplicate certificates are readily obtainable. Upon the presentation of these for the issue of passports or in demanding protection of the Government, the fraud sometimes escapes notice, and such certificates are not infrequently used in transactions of business to the deception and injury of innocent parties. Without placing any additional obstacles in the way of the obtainment of citizenship by the worthy and well-intentioned foreigner who comes in good faith to cast his lot with ours, I earnestly recommend further legislation to punish fraudulent naturalization and to secure the ready cancellation of the record of every naturalization made in fraud.

Since my last annual message the exchange has been made of the ratification of treaties of extradition with Belgium, Ecuador, Peru, and Salvador; also of a treaty of commerce and navigation with Peru, and one of commerce and consular privileges with Salvador; all of which have been duly proclaimed, as has also a declaration with Russia with reference to trade-marks.

The report of the Secretary of the Treasury, which by law is made directly to Congress, and forms no part of this message, will show the receipts and expenditures of the Government for the last fiscal year, the amount received from each source of revenue, and the amount paid out for each of the Departments of Government. It will be observed from this report that the amount of receipts over expenditures has been but $2,344,882.30 for the fiscal year ending June 30, 1874, and that for the current fiscal year the estimated receipts over expenditures will not much exceed $9,000,000. In view of the large national debt existing and the obligation to add 1 per cent per annum to the sinking fund, a sum amounting now to over $34,000,000 per annum, I submit whether revenues should not be increased or expenditures diminished to reach this amount of surplus. Not to provide for the sinking fund is a partial failure to comply with the contracts and obligations of the Government. At the last session of Congress a very considerable reduction was made in rates of taxation and in the number of articles submitted to taxation; the question may well be asked, whether or not, in some instances, unwisely. In connection with this subject, too, I venture the opinion that the means of collecting the revenue, especially from imports, have been so embarrassed by legislation as to make it questionable whether or not large amounts are not lost by failure to collect, to the direct loss of the Treasury and to the prejudice of the interests of honest importers and taxpayers.

The Secretary of the Treasury in his report favors legislation looking to an early return to specie payments, thus supporting views previously expressed in this message. He also recommends economy in appropriations; calls attention to the loss of revenue from repealing the tax on tea and coffee, without benefit to the consumer; recommends an increase of 10 cents a gallon on whisky, and, further, that no modification be made in the banking and currency bill passed at the last session of Congress, unless modification should become necessary by reason of the adoption of measures for returning to specie payments. In these recommendations I cordially join.

I would suggest to Congress the propriety of readjusting the tariff so as to increase the revenue, and at the same time decrease the number of articles upon which duties are levied. Those articles which enter into our manufactures and are not produced at home, it seems to me, should be entered free. Those articles of manufacture which we produce a constituent part of, but do not produce the whole, that part which we do not produce should enter free also. I will instance fine wool, dyes, etc. These articles must be imported to form a part of the manufacture of the higher grades of woolen goods. Chemicals used as dyes, compounded in medicines, and used in various ways in manufactures come under this class. The introduction free of duty of such wools as we do not produce would stimulate the manufacture of goods requiring the use of those we do produce, and therefore would be a benefit to home production. There are many articles entering into "home manufactures" which we do not produce ourselves the tariff upon which increases the cost of producing the manufactured article. All corrections in this regard are in the direction of bringing labor and capital in harmony with each other and of supplying one of the elements of prosperity so much needed.

The report of the Secretary of War herewith attached, and forming a part of this message, gives all the information concerning the operations, wants, and necessities of the Army, and contains many suggestions and recommendations which I commend to your special attention.

There is no class of Government employees who are harder worked than the Army—officers and men; none who perform their tasks more cheerfully and efficiently and under circumstances of greater privations and hardships.

Legislation is desirable to render more efficient this branch of the public service. All the recommendations of the Secretary of War I regard as judicious, and I especially commend to your attention the following: The consolidation of Government arsenals; the restoration of mileage to officers traveling under orders; the exemption of money received from the sale of subsistence stores from being covered into the Treasury; the use of appropriations for the purchase of subsistence stores without waiting for the beginning of the fiscal year for which the appropriation is made; for additional appropriations for the collection of torpedo material; for increased appropriations for the manufacture of arms; for relieving the various States from indebtedness for arms charged to them during the rebellion; for dropping officers from the rolls of the Army without trial for the offense of drawing pay more than once for the same period; for the discouragement of the plan to pay soldiers by cheek, and for the establishment of a professorship of rhetoric and English literature at West Point. The reasons for these recommendations are obvious, and are set forth sufficiently in the reports attached. I also recommend that the status of the staff corps of the Army be fixed, where this has not already been done, so that promotions may be made and vacancies filled as they occur in each grade when reduced below the number to be fixed by law. The necessity for such legislation is specially felt now in the Pay Department. The number of officers in that department is below the number adequate to the performance of the duties required of them by law.

The efficiency of the Navy has been largely increased during the last year. Under the impulse of the foreign complications which threatened us at the commencement of the last session of Congress, most of our efficient wooden ships were put in condition for immediate service, and the repairs of our ironclad fleet were pushed with the utmost vigor. The result is that most of these are now in an effective state and need only to be manned and put in commission to go at once into service.

Some of the new sloops authorized by Congress are already in commission, and most of the remainder are launched and wait only the completion of their machinery to enable them to take their places as part of our effective force.

Two iron torpedo ships have been completed during the last year, and four of our large double-turreted ironclads are now undergoing repairs. When these are finished, everything that is useful of our Navy, as now authorized, will be in condition for service, and with the advance in the science of torpedo warfare the American Navy, comparatively small as it is, will be found at any time powerful for the purposes of a peaceful nation.

Much has been accomplished during the year in aid of science and to increase the sum of general knowledge and further the interests of commerce and civilization. Extensive and much-needed soundings have been made for hydrographic purposes and to fix the proper routes of ocean telegraphs. Further surveys of the great Isthmus have been undertaken and completed, and two vessels of the Navy are now employed, in conjunction with those of England, France, Germany, and Russia, in observations connected with the transit of Venus, so useful and interesting to the scientific world.

The estimates for this branch of the public service do not differ materially from those of last year, those for the general support of the service being somewhat less and those for permanent improvements at the various stations rather larger than the corresponding estimate made a year ago. The regular maintenance and a steady increase in the efficiency of this most important arm in proportion to the growth of our maritime intercourse and interests is recommended to the attention of Congress.

The use of the Navy in time of peace might be further utilized by a direct authorization of the employment of naval vessels in explorations and surveys of the supposed navigable waters of other nationalities on this continent, especially the tributaries of the two great rivers of South America, the Orinoco and the Amazon. Nothing prevents, under existing laws, such exploration, except that expenditures must be made in such expeditions beyond those usually provided for in the appropriations. The field designated is unquestionably one of interest and one capable of large development of commercial interests—advantageous to the peoples reached and to those who may establish relations with them.

Education of the people entitled to exercise the right of franchise I regard essential to general prosperity everywhere, and especially so in republics, where birth, education, or previous condition does not enter into account in giving suffrage. Next to the public school, the post-office is the great agent of education over our vast territory. The rapidity with which new sections are being settled, thus increasing the carrying of mails in a more rapid ratio than the increase of receipts, is not alarming. The report of the Postmaster-General herewith attached shows that there was an increase of revenue in his Department in 1873 over the previous year of $1,674,411, and an increase of cost of carrying the mails and paying employees of $3,041,468.91. The report of the Postmaster-General gives interesting statistics of his Department, and compares them with the corresponding statistics of a year ago, showing a growth in every branch of the Department.

A postal convention has been concluded with New South Wales, an exchange of postal cards established with Switzerland, and the negotiations pending for several years past with France have been terminated in a convention with that country, which went into effect last August.

An international postal congress was convened in Berne, Switzerland, in September last, at which the United States was represented by an officer of the Post-Office Department of much experience and of qualification for the position. A convention for the establishment of an international postal union was agreed upon and signed by the delegates of the countries represented, subject to the approval of the proper authorities of those countries.

I respectfully direct your attention to the report of the Postmaster-General and to his suggestions in regard to an equitable adjustment of the question of compensation to railroads for carrying the mails.

Your attention will be drawn to the unsettled condition of affairs in some of the Southern States.

On the 14th of September last the governor of Louisiana called upon me, as provided by the Constitution and laws of the United States, to aid in suppressing domestic violence in that State. This call was made in view of a proclamation issued on that day by D. B. Penn, claiming that he was elected lieutenant-governor in 1872, and calling upon the militia of the State to arm, assemble, and drive from power the usurpers, as he designated the officers of the State government. On the next day I issued my proclamation commanding the insurgents to disperse within five days from the date thereof, and subsequently learned that on that day they had taken forcible possession of the statehouse. Steps were taken by me to support the existing and recognized State government, but before the expiration of the five days the insurrectionary movement was practically abandoned, and the officers of the State government, with some minor exceptions, resumed their powers and duties. Considering that the present State administration of Louisiana has been the only government in that State for nearly two years; that it has been tacitly acknowledged and acquiesced in as such by Congress, and more than once expressly recognized by me, I regarded it as my clear duty, when legally called upon for that purpose, to prevent its overthrow by an armed mob under pretense of fraud and irregularity in the election of 1872. I have heretofore called the attention of Congress to this subject, stating that on account of the frauds and forgeries committed at said election, and because it appears that the returns thereof were never legally canvassed, it was impossible to tell thereby who were chosen; but from the best sources of information at my command I have always believed that the present State officers received a majority of the legal votes actually cast at that election. I repeat what I said in my special message of February 23, 1873, that in the event of no action by Congress I must continue to recognize the government heretofore recognized by me.

I regret to say that with preparations for the late election decided indications appeared in some localities in the Southern States of a determination, by acts of violence and intimidation, to deprive citizens of the freedom of the ballot because of their political opinions. Bands of men, masked and armed, made their appearance; White Leagues and other societies were formed; large quantities of arms and ammunition were imported and distributed to these organizations; military drills, with menacing demonstrations, were held, and with all these murders enough were committed to spread terror among those whose political action was to be suppressed, if possible, by these intolerant and criminal proceedings. In some places colored laborers were compelled to vote according to the wishes of their employers, under threats of discharge if they acted otherwise; and there are too many instances in which, when these threats were disregarded, they were remorselessly executed by those who made them. I understand that the fifteenth amendment to the Constitution was made to prevent this and a like state of things, and the act of May 31, 1870, with amendments, was passed to enforce its provisions, the object of both being to guarantee to all citizens the right to vote and to protect them in the free enjoyment of that right. Enjoined by the Constitution "to take care that the laws be faithfully executed," and convinced by undoubted evidence that violations of said act had been committed and that a widespread and flagrant disregard of it was contemplated, the proper officers were instructed to prosecute the offenders, and troops were stationed at convenient points to aid these officers, if necessary, in the performance of their official duties. Complaints are made of this interference by Federal authority; but if said amendment and act do not provide for such interference under the circumstances as above stated, then they are without meaning, force, or effect, and the whole scheme of colored enfranchisement is worse than mockery and little better than a crime. Possibly Congress may find it due to truth and justice to ascertain, by means of a committee, whether the alleged wrongs to colored citizens for political purposes are real or the reports thereof were manufactured for the occasion.

The whole number of troops in the States of Louisiana, Alabama, Georgia, Florida, South Carolina, North Carolina, Kentucky, Tennessee, Arkansas, Mississippi, Maryland, and Virginia at the time of the election was 4,082. This embraces the garrisons of all the forts from the Delaware to the Gulf of Mexico.

Another trouble has arisen in Arkansas. Article 13 of the constitution of that State (which was adopted in 1868, and upon the approval of which by Congress the State was restored to representation as one of the States of the Union) provides in effect that before any amendments proposed to this constitution shall become a part thereof they shall be passed by two successive assemblies and then submitted to and ratified by a majority of the electors of the State voting thereon. On the 11th of May, 1874, the governor convened an extra session of the general assembly of the State, which on the 18th of the same month passed an act providing for a convention to frame a new constitution. Pursuant to this act, and at an election held on the 30th of June, 1874, the convention was approved, and delegates were chosen thereto, who assembled on the 14th of last July and framed a new constitution, the schedule of which provided for the election of an entire new set of State officers in a manner contrary to the then existing election laws of the State. On the 13th of October, 1874, this constitution, as therein provided, was submitted to the people for their approval or rejection, and according to the election returns was approved by a large majority of those qualified to vote thereon; and at the same election persons were chosen to fill all the State, county, and township offices. The governor elected in 1872 for the term of four years turned over his office to the governor chosen under the new constitution, whereupon the lieutenant-governor, also elected in 1872 for a term of four years, claiming to act as governor, and alleging that said proceedings by which the new constitution was made and a new set of officers elected were unconstitutional, illegal, and void, called upon me, as provided in section 4, Article IV, of the Constitution, to protect the State against domestic violence. As Congress is now investigating the political affairs of Arkansas, I have declined to interfere.

The whole subject of Executive interference with the affairs of a State is repugnant to public opinion, to the feelings of those who, from their official capacity, must be used in such interposition, and to him or those who must direct. Unless most clearly on the side of law, such interference becomes a crime; with the law to support it, it is condemned without a heating. I desire, therefore, that all necessity for Executive direction in local affairs may become unnecessary and obsolete. I invite the attention, not of Congress, but of the people of the United States, to the causes and effects of these unhappy questions. Is there not a disposition on one side to magnify wrongs and outrages, and on the other side to belittle them or justify them? If public opinion could be directed to a correct survey of what is and to rebuking wrong and aiding the proper authorities in punishing it, a better state of feeling would be inculcated, and the sooner we would have that peace which would leave the States free indeed to regulate their own domestic affairs. I believe on the part of our citizens of the Southern States—the better part of them—there is a disposition to be law abiding, and to do no violence either to individuals or to the laws existing. But do they do right in ignoring the existence of violence and bloodshed in resistance to constituted authority? I sympathize with their prostrate condition, and would do all in my power to relieve them, acknowledging that in some instances they have had most trying governments to live under, and very oppressive ones in the way of taxation for nominal improvements, not giving benefits equal to the hardships imposed. But can they proclaim themselves entirely irresponsible for this condition? They can not. Violence has been rampant in some localities, and has either been justified or denied by those who could have prevented it. The theory is even raised that there is to be no further interference on the part of the General Government to protect citizens within a State where the State authorities fail to give protection. This is a great mistake. While I remain Executive all the laws of Congress and the provisions of the Constitution, including the recent amendments added thereto, will be enforced with rigor, but with regret that they should have added one jot or tittle to Executive duties or powers. Let there be fairness in the discussion of Southern questions, the advocates of both or all political parties giving honest, truthful reports of occurrences, condemning the wrong and upholding the tight, and soon all will be well. Under existing conditions the negro votes the Republican ticket because he knows his friends are of that party. Many a good citizen votes the opposite, not because he agrees with the great principles of state which separate parties, but because, generally, he is opposed to negro rule. This is a most delusive cry. Treat the negro as a citizen and a voter, as he is and must remain, and soon parties will be divided, not on the color line, but on principle. Then we shall have no complaint of sectional interference.

The report of the Attorney-General contains valuable recommendations relating to the administration of justice in the courts of the United States, to which I invite your attention.

I respectfully suggest to Congress the propriety of increasing the number of judicial districts in the United States to eleven (the present number being nine) and the creation of two additional judgeships. The territory to be traversed by the circuit judges is so great and the business of the courts so steadily increasing that it is growing more and more impossible for them to keep up with the business requiring their attention. Whether this would involve the necessity of adding two more justices of the Supreme Court to the present number I submit to the judgment of Congress.

The attention of Congress is invited to the report of the Secretary of the Interior and to the legislation asked for by him. The domestic interests of the people are more intimately connected with this Department than with either of the other Departments of Government. Its duties have been added to from time to time until they have become so onerous that without the most perfect system and order it will be impossible for any Secretary of the Interior to keep trace of all official transactions having his sanction and done in his name, and for which he is held personally responsible.

The policy adopted for the management of Indian affairs, known as the peace policy, has been adhered to with most beneficial results. It is confidently hoped that a few years more will relieve our frontiers from danger of Indian depredations.

I commend the recommendation of the Secretary for the extension of the homestead laws to the Indians and for some sort of Territorial government for the Indian Territory. A great majority of the Indians occupying this Territory are believed yet to be incapable of maintaining their rights against the more civilized and enlightened white man. Any Territorial form of government given them, therefore, should protect them in their homes and property for a period of at least twenty years, and before its final adoption should be ratified by a majority of those affected.

The report of the Secretary of the Interior herewith attached gives much interesting statistical information, which I abstain from giving an abstract of, but refer you to the report itself.

The act of Congress providing the oath which pensioners must subscribe to before drawing their pensions cuts off from this bounty a few survivors of the War of 1812 residing in the Southern States. I recommend the restoration of this bounty to all such. The number of persons whose names would thus be restored to the list of pensioners is not large. They are all old persons, who could have taken no part in the rebellion, and the services for which they were awarded pensions were in defense of the whole country.

The report of the Commissioner of Agriculture herewith contains suggestions of much interest to the general public, and refers to the sly approaching Centennial and the part his Department is ready to take in it. I feel that the nation at large is interested in having this exposition a success, and commend to Congress such action as will secure a greater general interest in it. Already many foreign nations have signified their intention to be represented at it, and it may be expected that every civilized nation will be represented.

The rules adopted to improve the civil service of the Government have been adhered to as closely as has been practicable with the opposition with which they meet. The effect, I believe, has been beneficial on the whole, and has tended to the elevation of the service. But it is impracticable to maintain them without direct and positive support of Congress. Generally the support which this reform receives is from those who give it their support only to find fault when the rules are apparently departed from. Removals from office without preferring charges against parties removed are frequently cited as departures from the rules adopted, and the retention of those against whom charges are made by irresponsible persons and without good grounds is also often condemned as a violation of them. Under these circumstances, therefore, I announce that if Congress adjourns without positive legislation on the subject of "civil-service reform" I will regard such action as a disapproval of the system, and will abandon it, except so far as to require examinations for certain appointees, to determine their fitness. Competitive examinations will be abandoned.

The gentlemen who have given their services, without compensation, as members of the board to devise rules and regulations for the government of the civil service of the country have shown much zeal and earnestness in their work, and to them, as well as to myself, it will be a source of mortification if it is to be thrown away. But I repeat that it is impossible to carry this system to a successful issue without general approval and assistance and positive law to support it.

I have stated that three elements of prosperity to the nation—capital, labor, skilled and unskilled, and products of the soil—still remain with us. To direct the employment of these is a problem deserving the most serious attention of Congress. If employment can be given to all the labor offering itself, prosperity necessarily follows. I have expressed the opinion, and repeat it, that the first requisite to the accomplishment of this end is the substitution of a sound currency in place of one of a fluctuating value. This secured, there are many interests that might be fostered to the great profit of both labor and capital. How to induce capital to employ labor is the question. The subject of cheap transportation has occupied the attention of Congress. Much new light on this question will without doubt be given by the committee appointed by the last Congress to investigate and report upon this subject.

A revival of shipbuilding, and particularly of iron steamship building, is of vast importance to our national prosperity. The United States is now paying over $100,000,000 per annum for freights and passage on foreign ships—to be carried abroad and expended in the employment and support of other peoples—beyond a fair percentage of what should go to foreign vessels, estimating on the tonnage and travel of each respectively. It is to be regretted that this disparity in the carrying trade exists, and to correct it I would be willing to see a great departure from the usual course of Government in supporting what might usually be termed private enterprise. I would not suggest as a remedy direct subsidy to American steamship lines, but I would suggest the direct offer of ample compensation for carrying the mails between Atlantic Seaboard cities and the Continent on American-owned and American-built steamers, and would extend this liberality to vessels carrying the mails to South American States and to Central America and Mexico, and would pursue the same policy from our Pacific seaports to foreign seaports on the Pacific. It might be demanded that vessels built for this service should come up to a standard fixed by legislation in tonnage, speed, and all other qualities, looking to the possibility of Government requiring them at some time for war purposes. The right also of taking possession of them in such emergency should be guarded.

I offer these suggestions, believing them worthy of consideration, in all seriousness, affecting all sections and all interests alike. If anything better can be done to direct the country into a course of general prosperity, no one will be more ready than I to second the plan.

Forwarded herewith will be found the report of the commissioners appointed under an act of Congress approved June 20, 1874, to wind up the affairs of the District government. It will be seen from the report that the net debt of the District of Columbia, less securities on hand and available, is:

Bonded debt issued prior to July 1, 1874 - - $8,883,940.93
3.65 bonds, act of Congress June 20, 1874 - - 2,088,168.73

Certificates of the board of audit - - 4,770,558.45

December 7, 1875
To the Senate and House of Representatives:

In submitting my seventh annual message to Congress, in this centennial year of our national existence as a free and independent people, it affords me great pleasure to recur to the advancement that has been made from the time of the colonies, one hundred years ago. We were then a people numbering only 3,000,000. Now we number more than 40,000,000. Then industries were confined almost exclusively to the tillage of the soil. Now manufactories absorb much of the labor of the country.

Our liberties remain unimpaired; the bondmen have been freed from slavery; we have become possessed of the respect, if not the friendship, of all civilized nations. Our progress has been great in all the arts—in science, agriculture, commerce, navigation, mining, mechanics, law, medicine, etc.; and in general education the progress is likewise encouraging. Our thirteen States have become thirty-eight, including Colorado (which has taken the initiatory steps to become a State), and eight Territories, including the Indian Territory and Alaska, and excluding Colorado, making a territory extending from the Atlantic to the Pacific. On the south we have extended to the Gulf of Mexico, and in the west from the Mississippi to the Pacific.

One hundred years ago the cotton gin, the steamship, the railroad, the telegraph, the reaping, sewing, and modern printing machines, and numerous other inventions of scarcely less value to our business and happiness were entirely unknown.

In 1776 manufactories scarcely existed even in name in all this vast territory. In 1870 more than 2,000,000 persons were employed in manufactories, producing more than $2,100,000,000 of products in amount annually, nearly equal to our national debt. From nearly the whole of the population of 1776 being engaged in the one occupation of agriculture, in 1870 so numerous and diversified had become the occupation of our people that less than 6,000,000 out of more than 40,000,000 were so engaged. The extraordinary effect produced in our country by a resort to diversified occupations has built a market for the products of fertile lands distant from the seaboard and the markets of the world.

The American system of locating various and extensive manufactories next to the plow and the pasture, and adding connecting railroads and steamboats, has produced in our distant interior country a result noticeable by the intelligent portions of all commercial nations. The ingenuity and skill of American mechanics have been demonstrated at home and abroad in a manner most flattering to their pride. But for the extraordinary genius and ability of our mechanics, the achievements of our agriculturists, manufacturers, and transporters throughout the country would have been impossible of attainment.

The progress of the miner has also been great. Of coal our production has small; now many millions of tons are mined annually. So with iron, which formed scarcely an appreciable part of our products half a century ago, we now produce more than the world consumed at the beginning of our national existence. Lead, zinc, and copper, from being articles of import, we may expect to be large exporters of in the near future. The development of gold and silver mines in the United States and Territories has not only been remarkable, but has had a large influence upon the business of all commercial nations. Our merchants in the last hundred years have had a success and have established a reputation for enterprise, sagacity, progress, and integrity unsurpassed by peoples of older nationalities. This "good name" is not confined to their homes, but goes out upon every sea and into every port where commerce enters. With equal pride we can point to our progress in all of the learned professions.

As we are now about to enter upon our second centennial—commenting our manhood as a nation—it is well to look back upon the past and study what will be best to preserve and advance our future greatness From the fall of Adam for his transgression to the present day no nation has ever been free from threatened danger to its prosperity and happiness. We should look to the dangers threatening us, and remedy them so far as lies in our power. We are a republic whereof one man is as good as another before the law. Under such a form of government it is of the greatest importance that all should be possessed of education and intelligence enough to cast a vote with a right understanding of its meaning. A large association of ignorant men can not for any considerable period oppose a successful resistance to tyranny and oppression from the educated few, but will inevitably sink into acquiescence to the will of intelligence, whether directed by the demagogue or by priestcraft. Hence the education of the masses becomes of the first necessity for the preservation of our institutions. They are worth preserving, because they have secured the greatest good to the greatest proportion of the population of any form of government yet devised. All other forms of government approach it just in proportion to the general diffusion of education and independence of thought and action. As the primary step, therefore, to our advancement in all that has marked our progress in the past century, I suggest for your earnest consideration, and most earnestly recommend it, that a constitutional amendment be submitted to the legislatures of the several States for ratification, making it the duty of each of the several States to establish and forever maintain free public schools adequate to the education of all the children in the rudimentary branches within their respective limits, irrespective of sex, color, birthplace, or religions; forbidding the teaching in said schools of religious, atheistic, or pagan tenets; and prohibiting the granting of any school funds or school taxes, or any part thereof, either by legislative, municipal, or other authority, for the benefit or in aid, directly or indirectly, of any religious sect or denomination, or in aid or for the benefit of any other object of any nature or kind whatever.

In connection with this important question I would also call your attention to the importance of correcting an evil that, if permitted to continue, will probably lead to great trouble in our land before the close of the nineteenth century. It is the accumulation of vast amounts of untaxed church property. In 1850, I believe, the church property of the United States which paid no tax, municipal or State, amounted to about $83,000,000. In 1860 the amount had doubled; in 1875 it is about $1,000,000,000. By 1900, without check, it is safe to say this property will reach a sum exceeding $3,000,000,000. So vast a sum, receiving all the protection and benefits of Government without bearing its proportion of the burdens and expenses of the same, will not be looked upon acquiescently by those who have to pay the taxes. In a growing country, where real estate enhances so rapidly with time as in the United States, there is scarcely a limit to the wealth that may be acquired by corporations, religious or otherwise, if allowed to retain real estate without taxation. The contemplation of so vast a property as here alluded to, without taxation, may lead to sequestration without constitutional authority and through blood.

I would suggest the taxation of all property equally, whether church or corporation, exempting only the last resting place of the dead and possibly, with proper restrictions, church edifices.

Our relations with most of the foreign powers continue on a satisfactory and friendly footing.

Increased intercourse, the extension of commerce, and the cultivation of mutual interests have steadily improved our relations with the large majority of the powers of the world, rendering practicable the peaceful solution of questions which from time to time necessarily arise, leaving few which demand extended or particular notice.

The correspondence of the Department of State with our diplomatic representatives abroad is transmitted herewith.

I am happy to announce the passage of an act by the General Cortes of Portugal, proclaimed since the adjournment of Congress, for the abolition of servitude in the Portuguese colonies. It is to be hoped that such legislation may be another step toward the great consummation to be reached, when no man shall be permitted, directly or indirectly, under any guise, excuse, or form of law, to hold his fellow-man in bondage. I am of opinion also that it is the duty of the United States, as contributing toward that end, and required by the spirit of the age in which we live, to provide by suitable legislation that no citizen of the United States shall hold slaves as property in any other country or be interested therein.

Chile has made reparation in the case of the whale ship Good Return, seized without sufficient cause upward of forty years ago. Though she had hitherto denied her accountability, the denial was never acquiesced in by this Government, and the justice of the claim has been so earnestly contended for that it has been gratifying that she should have at last acknowledged it.

The arbitrator in the case of the United States steamer Montijo, for the seizure and detention of which the Government of the United States of Colombia was held accountable, has decided in favor of the claim. This decision has settled a question which had been pending for several years, and which, while it continued open, might more or less disturb the good understanding which it is desirable should be maintained between the two Republics.

A reciprocity treaty with the King of the Hawaiian Islands was concluded some months since. As it contains a stipulation that it shall not take effect until Congress shall enact the proper legislation for that purpose, copies of the instrument are herewith submitted, in order that, if such should be the pleasure of Congress, the necessary legislation upon the subject may be adopted.

In March last an arrangement was made, through Mr. Cushing, our minister in Madrid, with the Spanish Government for the payment by the latter to the United States of the sum of $80,000 in coin, for the purpose of the relief of the families or persons of the ship's company and certain passengers of the Virginius. This sum was to have been paid in three installments at two months each. It is due to the Spanish Government that I should state that the payments were fully and spontaneously anticipated by that Government, and that the whole amount was paid within but a few days more than two months from the date of the agreement, a copy of which is herewith transmitted. In pursuance of the terms of the adjustment, I have directed the distribution of the amount among the parties entitled thereto, including the ship's company and such of the passengers as were American citizens. Payments are made accordingly, on the application by the parties entitled thereto.

The past year has furnished no evidence of an approaching termination of the ruinous conflict which has been raging for seven years in the neighboring island of Cuba. The same disregard of the laws of civilized warfare and of the just demands of humanity which has heretofore called forth expressions of condemnation from the nations of Christendom has continued to blacken the sad scene. Desolation, ruin, and pillage are pervading the rich fields of one of the most fertile and productive regions of the earth, and the incendiary's torch, firing plantations and valuable factories and buildings, is the agent marking the alternate advance or retreat of contending parties.

The protracted continuance of this strife seriously affects the interests of all commercial nations, but those of the United States more than others, by reason of close proximity, its larger trade and intercourse with Cuba, and the frequent and intimate personal and social relations which have grown up between its citizens and those of the island. Moreover, the property of our citizens in Cuba is large, and is rendered insecure and depreciated in value and in capacity of production by the continuance of the strife and the unnatural mode of its conduct. The same is true, differing only in degree, with respect to the interests and people of other nations; and the absence of any reasonable assurance of a near termination of the conflict must of necessity soon compel the States thus suffering to consider what the interests of their own people and their duty toward themselves may demand.

I have hoped that Spain would be enabled to establish peace in her colony, to afford security to the property and the interests of our citizens, and allow legitimate scope to trade and commerce and the natural productions of the island. Because of this hope, and from an extreme reluctance to interfere in the most remote manner in the affairs of another and a friendly nation, especially of one whose sympathy and friendship in the struggling infancy of our own existence must ever be remembered with gratitude, I have patiently and anxiously waited the progress of events. Our own civil conflict is too recent for us not to consider the difficulties which surround a government distracted by a dynastic rebellion at home at the same time that it has to cope with a separate insurrection in a distant colony. But whatever causes may have produced the situation which so grievously affects our interests, it exists, with all its attendant evils operating directly upon this country and its people. Thus far all the efforts of Spain have proved abortive, and time has marked no improvement in the situation. The armed bands of either side now occupy nearly the same ground as in the past, with the difference, from time to time, of more lives sacrificed, more property destroyed, and wider extents of fertile and productive fields and more and more of valuable property constantly wantonly sacrificed to the incendiary's torch.

In contests of this nature, where a considerable body of people who have attempted to free themselves of the control of the superior government have reached such point in occupation of territory, in power, and in general organization as to constitute in fact a body politic; having a government in substance as well as in name; possessed of the elements of stability and equipped with the machinery for the administration of internal policy and the execution of its laws; prepared and able to administer justice at home, as well as in its dealings with other powers, it is within the province of those other powers to recognize its existence as a new and independent nation. In such cases other nations simply deal with an actually existing condition of things, and recognize as one of the powers of the earth that body politic which, possessing the necessary elements, has in fact become a new power. In a word, the creation of a new state is a fact.

To establish the condition of things essential to the recognition of this fact there must be a people occupying a known territory, united under some known and defined form of government, acknowledged by those subject thereto, in which the functions of government are administered by usual methods, competent to mete out justice to citizens and strangers, to afford remedies for public and for private wrongs, and able to assume the correlative international obligations and capable of performing the corresponding international duties resulting from its acquisition of the rights of sovereignty. A power should exist complete in its organization, ready to take and able to maintain its place among the nations of the earth.

While conscious that the insurrection in Cuba has shown a strength and endurance which make it at least doubtful whether it be in the power of Spain to subdue it, it seems unquestionable that no such civil organization exists which may be recognized as an independent government capable of performing its international obligations and entitled to be treated as one of the powers of the earth. A recognition under such circumstances would be inconsistent with the facts, and would compel the power granting it soon to support by force the government to which it had really given its only claim of existence. In my judgment the United States should adhere to the policy and the principles which have heretofore been its sure and safe guides in like contests between revolted colonies and their mother country, and, acting only upon the clearest evidence, should avoid any possibility of suspicion or of imputation.

A recognition of the independence of Cuba being, in my opinion, impracticable and indefensible, the question which next presents itself is that of the recognition of belligerent rights in the parties to the contest.

In a former message to Congress I had occasion to consider this question, and reached the conclusion that the conflict in Cuba, dreadful and devastating as were its incidents, did not rise to the fearful dignity of war. Regarding it now, after this lapse of time, I am unable to see that any notable success or any marked or real advance on the part of the insurgents has essentially changed the character of the contest. It has acquired greater age, but not greater or more formidable proportions. It is possible that the acts of foreign powers, and even acts of Spain herself, of this very nature, might be pointed to in defense of such recognition. But now, as in its past history, the United States should carefully avoid the false lights which might lead it into the mazes of doubtful law and of questionable propriety, and adhere rigidly and sternly to the rule, which has been its guide, of doing only that which is right and honest and of good report. The question of according or of withholding rights of belligerency must be judged in every case in view of the particular attending facts. Unless justified by necessity, it is always, and justly, regarded as an unfriendly act and a gratuitous demonstration of moral support to the rebellion. It is necessary, and it is required, when the interests and rights of another government or of its people are so far affected by a pending civil conflict as to require a definition of its relations to the parties thereto. But this conflict must be one which will be recognized in the sense of international law as war. Belligerence, too, is a fact. The mere existence of contending armed bodies and their occasional conflicts do not constitute war in the sense referred to. Applying to the existing condition of affairs in Cuba the tests recognized by publicists and writers on international law, and which have been observed by nations of dignity, honesty, and power when free from sensitive or selfish and unworthy motives, I fail to find in the insurrection the existence of such a substantial political organization, real, palpable, and manifest to the world, having the forms and capable of the ordinary functions of government toward its own people and to other states, with courts for the administration of justice, with a local habitation, possessing such organization of force, such material, such occupation of territory, as to take the contest out of the category of a mere rebellious insurrection or occasional skirmishes and place it on the terrible footing of war, to which a recognition of belligerency would aim to elevate it. The contest, moreover, is solely on land; the insurrection has not possessed itself of a single seaport whence it may send forth its flag, nor has it any means of communication with foreign powers except through the military lines of its adversaries. No apprehension of any of those sudden and difficult complications which a war upon the ocean is apt to precipitate upon the vessels, both commercial and national, and upon the consular officers of other powers calls for the definition of their relations to the parties to the contest. Considered as a question of expediency, I regard the accordance of belligerent rights still to be as unwise and premature as I regard it to be, at present, indefensible as a measure of right. Such recognition entails upon the country according the rights which flow from it difficult and complicated duties, and requires the exaction from the contending parties of the strict observance of their rights and obligations; it confers the right of search upon the high seas by vessels of both parties; it would subject the carrying of arms and munitions of war, which now may be transported freely and without interruption in the vessels of the United States, to detention and to possible seizure; it would give rise to countless vexatious questions, would release the parent Government from responsibility for acts done by the insurgents, and would invest Spain with the right to exercise the supervision recognized by our treaty of 1795 over our commerce on the high seas, a very large part of which, in its traffic between the Atlantic and the Gulf States and between all of them and the States on the Pacific, passes through the waters which wash the shores of Cuba. The exercise of this supervision could scarce fail to lead, if not to abuses, certainly to collisions perilous to the peaceful relations of the two States. There can be little doubt to what result such supervision would before long draw this nation. It would be unworthy of the United States to inaugurate the possibilities of such result by measures of questionable right or expediency or by any indirection. Apart from any question of theoretical right, I am satisfied that while the accordance of belligerent rights to the insurgents in Cuba might give them a hope and an inducement to protract the struggle, it would be but a delusive hope, and would not remove the evils which this Government and its people are experiencing, but would draw the United States into complications which it has waited long and already suffered much to avoid. The recognition of independence or of belligerency being thus, in my judgment, equally inadmissible, it remains to consider what course shall be adopted should the conflict not soon be brought to an end by acts of the parties themselves, and should the evils which result therefrom, affecting all nations, and particularly the United States, continue. In such event I am of opinion that other nations will be compelled to assume the responsibility which devolves upon them, and to seriously consider the only remaining measures possible—mediation and intervention, Owing, perhaps, to the large expanse of water separating the island from the peninsula, the want of harmony and of personal sympathy between the inhabitants of the colony and those sent thither to rule them, and want of adaptation of the ancient colonial system of Europe to the present times and to the ideas which the events of the past century have developed, the contending parties appear to have within themselves no depository of common confidence to suggest wisdom when passion and excitement have their sway and to assume the part of peacemaker. In this view in the earlier days of the contest the good offices of the United States as a mediator were tendered in good faith, without any selfish purpose, in the interest of humanity and in sincere friendship for both parties, but were at the time declined by Spain, with the declaration, nevertheless, that at a future time they would be indispensable. No intimation has been received that in the opinion of Spain that time has been reached. And yet the strife continues, with all its dread horrors and all its injuries to the interests of the United States and of other nations. Each party seems quite capable of working great injury and damage to the other, as well as to all the relations and interests dependent on the existence of peace in the island; but they seem incapable of reaching any adjustment, and both have thus far failed of achieving any success whereby one party shall possess and control the island to the exclusion of the other. Under these circumstances the agency of others, either by mediation or by intervention, seems to be the only alternative which must, sooner or later, be invoked for the termination of the strife. At the same time, while thus impressed I do not at this time recommend the adoption of any measure of intervention. I shall be ready at all times, and as the equal friend of both parties, to respond to a suggestion that the good offices of the United States will be acceptable to aid in bringing about a peace honorable to both. It is due to Spain, so far as this Government is concerned, that the agency of a third power, to which I have adverted, shall be adopted only as a last expedient. Had it been the desire of the United States to interfere in the affairs of Cuba, repeated opportunities for so doing have been presented within the last few years; but we have remained passive, and have performed our whole duty and all international obligations to Spain with friendship, fairness, and fidelity, and with a spirit of patience and forbearance which negatives every possible suggestion of desire to interfere or to add to the difficulties with which she has been surrounded.

The Government of Spain has recently submitted to our minister at Madrid certain proposals which it is hoped may be found to be the basis, if not the actual submission, of terms to meet the requirements of the particular griefs of which this Government has felt itself entitled to complain. These proposals have not yet reached me in their full text. On their arrival they will be taken into careful examination, and may, I hope, lead to a satisfactory adjustment of the questions to which they refer and remove the possibility of future occurrences such as have given rise to our just complaints.

It is understood also that renewed efforts are being made to introduce reforms in the internal administration of the island. Persuaded, however, that a proper regard for the interests of the United States and of its citizens entitles it to relief from the strain to which it has been subjected by the difficulties of the questions and the wrongs and losses which arise from the contest in Cuba, and that the interests of humanity itself demand the cessation of the strife before the whole island shall be laid waste and larger sacrifices of life be made, I shall feel it my duty, should my hopes of a satisfactory adjustment and of the early restoration of peace and the removal of future causes of complaint be, unhappily, disappointed, to make a further communication to Congress at some period not far remote, and during the present session, recommending what may then seem to me to be necessary.

The free zone, so called, several years since established by the Mexican Government in certain of the States of that Republic adjacent to our frontier, remains in full operation. It has always been materially injurious to honest traffic, for it operates as an incentive to traders in Mexico to supply without customs charges the wants of inhabitants on this side of the line, and prevents the same wants from being supplied by merchants of the United States, thereby to a considerable extent defrauding our revenue and checking honest commercial enterprise.

Depredations by armed bands from Mexico on the people of Texas near the frontier continue. Though the main object of these incursions is robbery, they frequently result in the murder of unarmed and peaceably disposed persons, and in some instances even the United States post-offices and mail communications have been attacked. Renewed remonstrances upon this subject have been addressed to the Mexican Government, but without much apparent effect. The military force of this Government disposable for service in that quarter is quite inadequate to effectually guard the line, even at those points where the incursions are usually made. An experiment of an armed vessel on the Rio Grande for that purpose is on trial, and it is hoped that, if not thwarted by the shallowness of the river and other natural obstacles, it may materially contribute to the protection of the herdsmen of Texas.

The proceedings of the joint commission under the convention between the United States and Mexico of the 4th of July, 1868, on the subject of claims, will soon be brought to a close. The result of those proceedings will then be communicated to Congress.

I am happy to announce that the Government of Venezuela has, upon further consideration, practically abandoned its objection to pay to the United States that share of its revenue which some years since it allotted toward the extinguishment of the claims of foreigners generally. In thus reconsidering its determination that Government has shown a just sense of self-respect which can not fail to reflect credit upon it in the eyes of all disinterested persons elsewhere. It is to be regretted, however, that its payments on account of claims of citizens of the United States are still so meager in amount, and that the stipulations of the treaty in regard to the sums to be paid and the periods when those payments were to take place should have been so signally disregarded.

Since my last annual message the exchange has been made of the ratification of a treaty of commerce and navigation with Belgium, and of conventions with the Mexican Republic for the further extension of the joint commission respecting claims; with the Hawaiian Islands for commercial reciprocity, and with the Ottoman Empire for extradition; all of which have been duly proclaimed.

The Court of Commissioners of Alabama Claims has prosecuted its important duties very assiduously and very satisfactorily. It convened and was organized on the 22d day of July, 1874, and by the terms of the act under which it was created was to exist for one year from that date. The act provided, however, that should it be found impracticable to complete the work of the court before the expiration of the year the President might by proclamation extend the time of its duration to a period not more than six months beyond the expiration of the one year.

Having received satisfactory evidence that it would be impracticable to complete the work within the time originally fixed, I issued a proclamation (a copy of which is presented herewith) extending the time of duration of the court for a period of six months from and after the 22d day of July last.

A report made through the clerk of the court (communicated herewith) shows the condition of the calendar on the 1st of November last and the large amount of work which has been accomplished. One thousand three hundred and eighty-two claims have been presented, of which 682 had been disposed of at the date of the report. I am informed that 170 cases were decided during the month of November. Arguments are being made and decisions given in the remaining cases with all the dispatch consistent with the proper consideration of the questions submitted. Many of these claims are in behalf of mariners, or depend on the evidence of mariners, whose absence has delayed the taking or the return of the necessary evidence.

It is represented to me that it will be impracticable for the court to finally dispose of all the cases before it within the present limit of its duration. Justice to the parties claimant, who have been at large expense in preparing their claims and obtaining the evidence in their support, suggests a short extension, to enable the court to dispose of all of the claims which have been presented.

I recommend the legislation which may be deemed proper to enable the court to complete the work before it.

I recommend that some suitable provision be made, by the creation of a special court or by conferring the necessary jurisdiction upon some appropriate tribunal, for the consideration and determination of the claims of aliens against the Government of the United States which have arisen within some reasonable limitation of time, or which may hereafter arise, excluding all claims barred by treaty provisions or otherwise. It has been found impossible to give proper consideration to these claims by the Executive Departments of the Government. Such a tribunal would afford an opportunity to aliens other than British subjects to present their claims on account of acts committed against their persons or property during the rebellion, as also to those subjects of Great Britain whose claims, having arisen subsequent to the 9th day of April, 1865, could not be presented to the late commission organized pursuant to the provisions of the treaty of Washington.

The electric telegraph has become an essential and indispensable agent in the transmission of business and social messages. Its operation on land, and within the limit of particular states, is necessarily under the control of the jurisdiction within which it operates. The lines on the high seas, however, are not subject to the particular control of any one government.

In 1869 a concession was granted by the French Government to a company which proposed to lay a cable from the shores of France to the United

States. At that time there was a telegraphic connection between the United States and the continent of Europe (through the possessions of Great Britain at either end of the line), under the control of an association which had, at large outlay of capital and at great risk, demonstrated the practicability of maintaining such means of communication. The cost of correspondence by this agency was great, possibly not too large at the time for a proper remuneration for so hazardous and so costly an enterprise. It was, however, a heavy charge upon a means of communication which the progress in the social and commercial intercourse of the world found to be a necessity, and the obtaining of this French concession showed that other capital than that already invested was ready to enter into competition, with assurance of adequate return for their outlay. Impressed with the conviction that the interests, not only of the people of the United States, but of the world at large, demanded, or would demand, the multiplication of such means of communication between separated continents, I was desirous that the proposed connection should be made; but certain provisions of this concession were deemed by me to be objectionable, particularly one which gave for a long term of years the exclusive right of telegraphic communication by submarine cable between the shores of France and the United States. I could not concede that any power should claim the right to land a cable on the shores of the United States and at the same time deny to the United States, or to its citizens or grantees, an equal fight to land a cable on its shores. The right to control the conditions for the laying of a cable within the jurisdictional waters of the United States, to connect our shores with those of any foreign state, pertains exclusively to the Government of the United States, under such limitations and conditions as Congress may impose. In the absence of legislation by Congress I was unwilling, on the one hand, to yield to a foreign state the right to say that its grantees might land on our shores while it denied a similar right to our people to land on its shores, and, on the other hand, I was reluctant to deny to the great interests of the world and of civilization the facilities of such communication as were proposed. I therefore withheld any resistance to the landing of the cable on condition that the offensive monopoly feature of the concession be abandoned, and that the right of any cable which may be established by authority of this Government to land upon French territory and to connect with French land lines and enjoy all the necessary facilities or privileges incident to the use thereof upon as favorable terms as any other company be conceded. As the result thereof the company in question renounced the exclusive privilege, and the representative of France was informed that, understanding this relinquishment to be construed as granting the entire reciprocity and equal facilities which had been demanded, the opposition to the landing of the cable was withdrawn. The cable, under this French concession, was landed in the month of July, 1869, and has been an efficient and valuable agent of communication between this country and the other continent. It soon passed under the control, however, of those who had the management of the cable connecting Great Britain with this continent, and thus whatever benefit to the public might have ensued from competition between the two lines was lost, leaving only the greater facilities of an additional line and the additional security in case of accident to one of them. But these increased facilities and this additional security, together with the control of the combined capital of the two companies, gave also greater power to prevent the future construction of other lines and to limit the control of telegraphic communication between the two continents to those possessing the lines already laid. Within a few months past a cable has been laid, known as the United States Direct Cable Company, connecting the United States directly with Great Britain. As soon as this cable was reported to be laid and in working order the rates of the then existing consolidated companies were greatly reduced. Soon, however, a break was announced in this new cable, and immediately the rates of the other line, which had been reduced, were again raised. This cable being now repaired, the rates appear not to be reduced by either line from those formerly charged by the consolidated companies.

There is reason to believe that large amounts of capital, both at home and abroad, are ready to seek profitable investment in the advancement of this useful and most civilizing means of intercourse and correspondence. They await, however, the assurance of the means and conditions on which they may safely be made tributary to the general good.

As these cable telegraph lines connect separate states, there are questions as to their organization and control which probably can be best, if not solely, settled by conventions between the respective states. In the absence, however, of international conventions on the subject, municipal legislation may secure many points which appear to me important, if not indispensable for the protection of the public against the extortions which may result from a monopoly of the right of operating cable telegrams or from a combination between several lines:

I. No line should be allowed to land on the shores of the United States under the concession from another power which does not admit the right of any other line or lines, formed in the United States, to land and freely connect with and operate through its land lines.

II. No line should be allowed to land on the shores of the United States which is not, by treaty stipulation with the government from whose shores it proceeds, or by prohibition in its charter, or otherwise to the satisfaction of this Government, prohibited from consolidating or amalgamating with any other cable telegraph line, or combining therewith for the purpose of regulating and maintaining the cost of telegraphing.

III. All lines should be bound to give precedence in the transmission of the official messages of the governments of the two countries between which it may be laid.

IV. A power should be reserved to the two governments, either conjointly or to each, as regards the messages dispatched from its shores, to fix a limit to the charges to be demanded for the transmission of messages.

I present this subject to the earnest consideration of Congress.

In the meantime, and unless Congress otherwise direct, I shall not oppose the landing of any telegraphic cable which complies with and assents to the points above enumerated, but will feel it my duty to prevent the landing of any which does not conform to the first and second points as stated, and which will not stipulate to concede to this Government the precedence in the transmission of its official messages and will not enter into a satisfactory arrangement with regard to its charges.

Among the pressing and important subjects to which, in my opinion, the attention of Congress should be directed are those relating to fraudulent naturalization and expatriation.

The United States, with great liberality, offers its citizenship to all who in good faith comply with the requirements of law. These requirements are as simple and upon as favorable terms to the emigrant as the high privilege to which he is admitted can or should permit. I do not propose any additional requirements to those which the law now demands; but the very simplicity and the want of unnecessary formality in our law have made fraudulent naturalization not infrequent, to the discredit and injury of all honest citizens, whether native or naturalized. Cases of this character are continually being brought to the notice of the Government by our representatives abroad, and also those of persons resident in other countries, most frequently those who, if they have remained in this country long enough to entitle them to become naturalized, have generally not much overpassed that period, and have returned to the country of their origin, where they reside, avoiding all duties to the United States by their absence, and claiming to be exempt from all duties to the country of their nativity and of their residence by reason of their alleged naturalization. It is due to this Government itself and to the great mass of the naturalized citizens who entirely, both in name and in fact, become citizens of the United States that the high privilege of citizenship of the United States should not be held by fraud or in derogation of the laws and of the good name of every honest citizen. On many occasions it has been brought to the knowledge of the Government that certificates of naturalization are held and protection or interference claimed by parties who admit that not only they were not within the United States at the time of the pretended naturalization, but that they have never resided in the United States; in others the certificate and record of the court show on their face that the person claiming to be naturalized had not resided the required time in the

United States; in others it is admitted upon examination that the requirements of law have not been complied with; in some cases, even, such certificates have been matter of purchase. These are not isolated cases, arising at rare intervals, but of common occurrence, and which are reported from all quarters of the globe. Such occurrences can not, and do not, fail to reflect upon the Government and injure all honest citizens. Such a fraud being discovered, however, there is no practicable means within the control of the Government by which the record of naturalization can be vacated; and should the certificate be taken up, as it usually is, by the diplomatic and consular representatives of the Government to whom it may have been presented, there is nothing to prevent the person claiming to have been naturalized from obtaining a new certificate from the court in place of that which has been taken from him.

The evil has become so great and of such frequent occurrence that I can not too earnestly recommend that some effective measures be adopted to provide a proper remedy and means for the vacating of any record thus fraudulently made, and of punishing the guilty parties to the transaction.

In this connection I refer also to the question of expatriation and the election of nationality.

The United States was foremost in upholding the right of expatriation, and was principally instrumental in overthrowing the doctrine of perpetual allegiance. Congress has declared the right of expatriation to be a natural and inherent right of all people; but while many other nations have enacted laws providing what formalities shall be necessary to work a change of allegiance, the United States has enacted no provisions of law and has in no respect marked out how and when expatriation may be accomplished by its citizens. Instances are brought to the attention of the Government where citizens of the United States, either naturalized or native born, have formally become citizens or subjects of foreign powers, but who, nevertheless, in the absence of any provisions of legislation on this question, when involved in difficulties or when it seems to be their interest, claim to be citizens of the United States and demand the intervention of a Government which they have long since abandoned and to which for years they have rendered no service nor held themselves in any way amenable.

In other cases naturalized citizens, immediately after naturalization, have returned to their native country; have become engaged in business; have accepted offices or pursuits inconsistent with American citizenship, and evidence no intent to return to the United States until called upon to discharge some duty to the country where they are residing, when at once they assert their citizenship and call upon the representatives of the Government to aid them in their unjust pretensions. It is but justice to all bona fide citizens that no doubt should exist on such questions, and that Congress should determine by enactment of law how expatriation may be accomplished and change of citizenship be established.

I also invite your attention to the necessity of regulating by law the status of American women who may marry foreigners, and of defining more fully that of children born in a foreign country of American parents who may reside abroad; and also of some further provision regulating or giving legal effect to marriages of American citizens contracted in foreign countries. The correspondence submitted herewith shows a few of the constantly occurring questions on these points presented to the consideration of the Government. There are few subjects to engage the attention of Congress on which more delicate relations or more important interests are dependent.

In the month of July last the building erected for the Department of State was taken possession of and occupied by that Department. I am happy to announce that the archives and valuable papers of the Government in the custody of that Department are now safely deposited and properly cared for.

The report of the Secretary of the Treasury shows the receipts from customs for the fiscal year ending June 30, 1874, to have been $163,103,833.69, and for the fiscal year ending June 30, 1875, to have been $157,267,722.35, a decrease for the last fiscal year of $5,936,111.34. Receipts from internal revenue for the year ending the 30th of June, 1874, were $102,409,784.90, and for the year ending June 30, 1875, $110,007,493.58; increase, $7,597,708.68.

The report also shows a complete history of the workings of the Department for the last year, and contains recommendations for reforms and for legislation which I concur in, but can not comment on so fully as I should like to do if space would permit, but will confine myself to a few suggestions which I look upon as vital to the best interests of the whole people—coming within the purview of "Treasury;" I mean specie resumption. Too much stress can not be laid upon this question, and I hope Congress may be induced, at the earliest day practicable, to insure the consummation of the act of the last Congress, at its last session, to bring about specie resumption "on and after the 1st of January, 1879," at furthest. It would be a great blessing if this could be consummated even at an earlier day.

Nothing seems to me more certain than that a full, healthy, and permanent reaction can not take place in favor of the industries and financial welfare of the country until we return to a measure of values recognized throughout the civilized world. While we use a currency not equivalent to this standard the world's recognized standard, specie, becomes a commodity like the products of the soil, the surplus seeking a market wherever there is a demand for it.

Under our present system we should want none, nor would we have any, were it not that customs dues must be paid in coin and because of the pledge to pay interest on the public debt in coin. The yield of precious metals would flow out for the purchase of foreign productions and the United States "hewers of wood and drawers of water," because of wiser legislation on the subject of finance by the nations with whom we have dealings. I am not prepared to say that I can suggest the best legislation to secure the end most heartily recommended. It will be a source of great gratification to me to be able to approve any measure of Congress looking effectively toward securing "resumption."

Unlimited inflation would probably bring about specie payments more speedily than any legislation looking to redemption of the legal-tenders in coin; but it would be at the expense of honor. The legal-tenders would have no value beyond settling present liabilities, or, properly speaking, repudiating them. They would buy nothing after debts were all settled.

There are a few measures which seem to me important in this connection and which I commend to your earnest consideration:

A repeal of so much of the legal-tender act as makes these notes receivable for debts contracted after a date to be fixed in the act itself, say not later than the 1st of January, 1877. We should then have quotations at real values, not fictitious ones. Gold would no longer be at a premium, but currency at a discount. A healthy reaction would set in at once, and with it a desire to make the currency equal to what it purports to be. The merchants, manufacturers, and tradesmen of every calling could do business on a fair margin of profit, the money to be received having an unvarying value. Laborers and all classes who work for stipulated pay or salary would receive more for their income, because extra profits would no longer be charged by the capitalists to compensate for the risk of a downward fluctuation in the value of the currency.

Second. That the Secretary of the Treasury be authorized to redeem, say, not to exceed $2,000,000 monthly of legal-tender notes, by issuing in their stead a long bond, bearing interest at the rate of 3.65 per cent per annum, of denominations ranging from $50 up to $1,000 each. This would in time reduce the legal-tender notes to a volume that could be kept afloat without demanding redemption in large sums suddenly.

Third. That additional power be given to the Secretary of the Treasury to accumulate gold for final redemption, either by increasing revenue, curtailing expenses, or both (it is preferable to do both); and I recommend that reduction of expenditures be made wherever it can be done without impairing Government obligations or crippling the due execution thereof. One measure for increasing the revenue—and the only one I think of—is the restoration of the duty on tea and coffee. These duties would add probably $18,000,000 to the present amount received from imports, and would in no way increase the prices paid for those articles by the consumers.

These articles are the products of countries collecting revenue from exports, and as we, the largest consumers, reduce the duties they proportionately increase them. With this addition to the revenue, many duties now collected, and which give but an insignificant return for the cost of collection, might be remitted, and to the direct advantage of consumers at home.

I would mention those articles which enter into manufactures of all sorts. All duty paid upon such articles goes directly to the cost of the article when manufactured here, and must be paid for by the consumers. These duties not only come from the consumers at home, but act as a protection to foreign manufacturers of the same completed articles in our own and distant markets.

I will suggest or mention another subject bearing upon the problem of "how to enable the Secretary of the Treasury to accumulate balances." It is to devise some better method of verifying claims against the Government than at present exists through the Court of Claims, especially those claims growing out of the late war. Nothing is more certain than that a very large percentage of the amounts passed and paid are either wholly fraudulent or are far in excess of the real losses sustained. The large amount of losses proven—on good testimony according to existing laws, by affidavits of fictitious or unscrupulous persons—to have been sustained on small farms and plantations are not only far beyond the possible yield of those places for any one year, but, as everyone knows who has had experience in tilling the soil and who has visited the scenes of these spoliations, are in many instances more than the individual claimants were ever worth, including their personal and real estate.

The report of the Attorney-General, which will be submitted to Congress at an early day, will contain a detailed history of awards made and of claim pending of the class here referred to.

The report of the Secretary of War, accompanying this message, gives a detailed account of Army operations for the year just passed, expenses for maintenance, etc., with recommendations for legislation to which I respectfully invite your attention. To some of these I invite special attention:

First. The necessity of making $300,000 of the appropriation for the Subsistence Department available before the beginning of the next fiscal year. Without this provision troops at points distant from supply production must either go without food or existing laws must be violated. It is not attended with cost to the Treasury.

Second. His recommendation for the enactment of a system of annuities for the families of deceased officers by voluntary deductions from the monthly pay of officers. This again is not attended with burden upon the

Treasury, and would for the future relieve much distress which every old army officer has witnessed in the past—of officers dying suddenly or being killed, leaving families without even the means of reaching their friends, if fortunate enough to have friends to aid them.

Third. The repeal of the law abolishing mileage, and a return to the old system.

Fourth. The trial with torpedoes under the Corps of Engineers, and appropriation for the same. Should war ever occur between the United States and any maritime power, torpedoes will be among if not the most effective and cheapest auxiliary for the defense of harbors, and also in aggressive operations, that we can have. Hence it is advisable to learn by experiment their best construction and application, as well as effect.

Fifth. A permanent organization for the Signal-Service Corps. This service has now become a necessity of peace as well as war, under the advancement made by the present able management.

Sixth. A renewal of the appropriation for compiling the official records of the war, etc.

The condition of our Navy at this time is a subject of satisfaction. It does not contain, it is true, any of the powerful cruising ironclads which make so much of the maritime strength of some other nations, but neither our continental situation nor our foreign policy requires that we should have a large number of ships of this character, while this situation and the nature of our ports combine to make those of other nations little dangerous to us under any circumstances.

Our Navy does contain, however, a considerable number of ironclads of the monitor class, which, though not properly cruisers, are powerful and effective for harbor defense and for operations near our own shores. Of these all the single-turreted ones, fifteen in number, have been substantially rebuilt, their rotten wooden beams replaced with iron, their hulls strengthened, and their engines and machinery thoroughly repaired, so that they are now in the most efficient condition and ready for sea as soon as they can be manned and put in commission.

The five double-turreted ironclads belonging to our Navy, by far the most powerful of our ships for fighting purposes, are also in hand undergoing complete repairs, and could be ready for sea in periods varying from four to six months. With these completed according to the present design and our two iron torpedo boats now ready, our ironclad fleet will be, for the purposes of defense at home, equal to any force that can readily be brought against it.

Of our wooden navy also cruisers of various sizes, to the number of about forty, including those now in commission, are in the Atlantic, and could be ready for duty as fast as men could be enlisted for those not already in commission. Of these, one-third are in effect new ships, and though some of the remainder need considerable repairs to their boilers and machinery, they all are, or can readily be made, effective.

This constitutes a fleet of more than fifty war ships, of which fifteen are ironclad, now in hand on the Atlantic coast. The Navy has been brought to this condition by a judicious and practical application of what could be spared from the current appropriations of the last few years and from that made to meet the possible emergency of two years ago. It has been done quietly, without proclamation or display, and though it has necessarily straitened the Department in its ordinary expenditure, and, as far as the ironclads are concerned, has added nothing to the cruising force of the Navy, yet the result is not the less satisfactory because it is to be found in a great increase of real rather than apparent force. The expenses incurred in the maintenance of an effective naval force in all its branches are necessarily large, but such force is essential to our position, relations, and character, and affects seriously the weight of our principles and policy throughout the whole sphere of national responsibilities.

The estimates for the regular support of this branch of the service for the next year amount to a little less in the aggregate than those made for the current year; but some additional appropriations are asked for objects not included in the ordinary maintenance of the Navy, but believed to be of pressing importance at this time. It would, in my opinion, be wise at once to afford sufficient means for the immediate completion of the five double-turreted monitors now undergoing repairs, which must otherwise advance slowly, and only as money can be spared from current expenses. Supplemented by these, our Navy, armed with the destructive weapons of modern warfare, manned by our seamen, and in charge of our instructed officers, will present a force powerful for the home purposes of a responsible though peaceful nation.

The report of the Postmaster-General herewith transmitted gives a full history of the workings of the Department for the year just past. It will be observed that the deficiency to be supplied from the General Treasury is increased over the amount required for the preceding year. In a country so vast in area as the United States, with large portions sparsely settled, it must be expected that this important service will be more or less a burden upon the Treasury for many years to come. But there is no branch of the public service which interests the whole people more than that of cheap and rapid transmission of the mails to every inhabited part of our territory. Next to the free school, the post-office is the great educator of the people, and it may well receive the support of the General Government.

The subsidy of $150,000 per annum given to vessels of the United States for carrying the mails between New York and Rio de Janeiro having ceased on the 30th day of September last, we are without direct mail facilities with the South American States. This is greatly to be regretted, and I do not hesitate to recommend the authorization of a renewal of that contract, and also that the service may be increased from monthly to semi-monthly trips. The commercial advantages to be gained by a direct line of American steamers to the South American States will far outweigh the expense of the service.

By act of Congress approved March 3, 1875, almost all matter, whether properly mail matter or not, may be sent any distance through the mails, in packages not exceeding 4 pounds in weight, for the sum of 16 cents per pound. So far as the transmission of real mail matter goes, this would seem entirely proper; but I suggest that the law be so amended as to exclude from the mails merchandise of all descriptions, and limit this transportation to articles enumerated, and which may be classed as mail matter proper.

The discovery of gold in the Black Hills, a portion of the Sioux Reservation, has had the effect to induce a large emigration of miners to that point. Thus far the effort to protect the treaty rights of the Indians to that section has been successful, but the next year will certainly witness a large increase of such emigration. The negotiations for the relinquishment of the gold fields having failed, it will be necessary for Congress to adopt some measures to relieve the embarrassment growing out of the causes named. The Secretary of the Interior suggests that the supplies now appropriated for the sustenance of that people, being no longer obligatory under the treaty of 1868, but simply a gratuity, may be issued or withheld at his discretion.

The condition of the Indian Territory, to which I have referred in several of my former annual messages, remains practically unchanged. The Secretary of the Interior has taken measures to obtain a full report of the condition of that Territory, and will make it the subject of a special report at an early day. It may then be necessary to make some further recommendation in regard to legislation for the government of that Territory.

The steady growth and increase of the business of the Patent Office indicates in some measure the progress of the industrial activity of the country. The receipts of the office are in excess of its expenditures, and the office generally is in a prosperous and satisfactory condition.

The report of the General Land Office shows that there were 2,459,601 acres less disposed of during this than during the last year. More than one-half of this decrease was in lands disposed of under the homestead and timber-culture laws. The cause of this decrease is supposed to be found in the grasshopper scourge and the droughts which prevailed so extensively in some of the frontier States and Territories during that time as to discourage and deter entries by actual settlers. The cash receipts were less by $690,322.23 than during the preceding year.

The entire surveyed area of the public domain is 680,253,094 acres, of which 26,077,531 acres were surveyed during the past year, leaving 1,154,471,762 acres still unsurveyed.

The report of the Commissioner presents many interesting suggestions in regard to the management and disposition of the public domain and the modification of existing laws, the apparent importance of which should insure for them the careful consideration of Congress.

The number of pensioners still continues to decrease, the highest number having been reached during the year ending June 30, 1873. During the last year 11,557 names were added to the rolls, and 12,977 were dropped therefrom, showing a net decrease of 1,420. But while the number of pensioners has decreased, the annual amount due on the pension rolls has increased $44,733.13. This is caused by the greatly increased average rate of pensions, which, by the liberal legislation of Congress, has increased from $90.26 in 1872 to $103.91 in 1875 to each invalid pensioner, an increase in the average rate of 15 per cent in the three years. During the year ending June 30, 1875, there was paid on account of pensions, including the expenses of disbursement, $29,683,116, being $910,632 less than was paid the preceding year. This reduction in amount of expenditures was produced by the decrease in the amount of arrearages due on allowed claims and on pensions the rate of which was increased by the legislation of the preceding session of Congress. At the close of the last fiscal year there were on the pension rolls 234,821 persons, of whom 210,363 were army pensioners, 105,478 being invalids and 104,885 widows and dependent relatives; 3,420 were navy pensioners, of whom 1,636 were invalids and 1,784 widows and dependent relatives; 21,038 were pensioners of the War of 1812, 15,875 of whom were survivors and 5,163 were widows.

It is estimated that $29,535,000 will be required for the payment of pensions for the next fiscal year, an amount $965,000 less than the estimate for the present year.

The geological explorations have been prosecuted with energy during the year, covering an area of about 40,000 square miles in the Territories of Colorado, Utah, and New Mexico, developing the agricultural and mineral resources and furnishing interesting scientific and topographical details of that region.

The method for the treatment of the Indians adopted at the beginning of my first term has been steadily pursued, and with satisfactory and encouraging results. It has been productive of evident improvement in the condition of that race, and will be continued, with only such modifications as further experience may indicate to be necessary.

The board heretofore appointed to take charge of the articles and materials pertaining to the War, the Navy, the Treasury, the Interior, and the Post-Office Departments, and the Department of Agriculture, the Smithsonian Institution, and the Commission of Food Fishes, to be contributed, under the legislation of last session, to the international exhibition to be held at Philadelphia during the centennial year 1876, has been diligent in the discharge of the duties which have devolved upon it; and the preparations so far made with the means at command give assurance that the governmental contribution will be made one of the marked characteristics of the exhibition. The board has observed commendable economy in the matter of the erection of a building for the governmental exhibit, the expense of which it is estimated will not exceed, say, $80,000. This amount has been withdrawn, under the law, from the appropriations of five of the principal Departments, which leaves some of those Departments without sufficient means to render their respective practical exhibits complete and satisfactory. The exhibition being an international one, and the Government being a voluntary contributor, it is my opinion that its contribution should be of a character, in quality and extent, to sustain the dignity and credit of so distinguished a contributor. The advantages to the country of a creditable display are, in an international point of view, of the first importance, while an indifferent or uncreditable participation by the Government would be humiliating to the patriotic feelings of our people themselves. I commend the estimates of the board for the necessary additional appropriations to the favorable consideration of Congress.

The powers of Europe almost without exception, many of the South American States, and even the more distant Eastern powers have manifested their friendly sentiments toward the United States and the interest of the world in our progress by taking steps to join with us in celebrating the centennial of the nation, and I strongly recommend that a more national importance be given to this exhibition by such legislation and by such appropriation as will insure its success. Its value in bringing to our shores innumerable useful works of art and skill, the commingling of the citizens of foreign countries and our own, and the interchange of ideas and manufactures will far exceed any pecuniary outlay we may make.

I transmit herewith the report of the Commissioner of Agriculture, together with the reports of the Commissioners, the board of audit, and the board of health of the District of Columbia, to all of which I invite your attention.

The Bureau of Agriculture has accomplished much in disseminating useful knowledge to the agriculturist, and also in introducing new and useful productions adapted to our soil and climate, and is worthy of the continued encouragement of the Government.

The report of the Commissioner of Education, which accompanies the report of the Secretary of the Interior, shows a gratifying progress in educational matters.

In nearly every annual message that I have had the honor of transmitting to Congress I have called attention to the anomalous, not to say scandalous, condition of affairs existing in the Territory of Utah, and have asked for definite legislation to correct it. That polygamy should exist in a free, enlightened, and Christian country, without the power to punish so flagrant a crime against decency and morality, seems preposterous. True, there is no law to sustain this unnatural vice; but what is needed is a law to punish it as a crime, and at the same time to fix the status of the innocent children, the offspring of this system, and of the possibly innocent plural wives. But as an institution polygamy should be banished from the land.

While this is being done I invite the attention of Congress to another, though perhaps no less an evil—the importation of Chinese women, but few of whom are brought to our shores to pursue honorable or useful occupations.

Observations while visiting the Territories of Wyoming, Utah, and Colorado during the past autumn convinced me that existing laws regulating the disposition of public lands, timber, etc., and probably the mining laws themselves, are very defective and should be carefully amended, and at an early day. Territory where cultivation of the soil can only be followed by irrigation, and where irrigation is not practicable the lands can only be used as pasturage, and this only where stock can reach water (to quench its thirst), can not be governed by the same laws as to entries as lands every acre of which is an independent estate by itself.

Land must be held in larger quantities to justify the expense of conducting water upon it to make it fruitful, or to justify utilizing it as pasturage. The timber in most of the Territories is principally confined to the mountain regions, which are held for entry in small quantities only, and as mineral lands. The timber is the property of the United States, for the disposal of which there is now no adequate law. The settler must become a consumer of this timber, whether he lives upon the plain or engages in working the mines. Hence every man becomes either a trespasser himself or knowingly a patron of trespassers.

My opportunities for observation were not sufficient to justify me in recommending specific legislation on these subjects, but I do recommend that a joint committee of the two Houses of Congress, sufficiently large to be divided into subcommittees, be organized to visit all the mining States and Territories during the coming summer, and that the committee shall report to Congress at the next session such laws or amendments to laws as it may deem necessary to secure the best interests of the Government and the people of these Territories, who are doing so much for their development.

I am sure the citizens occupying the territory described do not wish to be trespassers, nor will they be if legal ways are provided for them to become owners of these actual necessities of their position.

As this will be the last annual message which I shall have the honor of transmitting to Congress before my successor is chosen, I will repeat or recapitulate the questions which I deem of vital importance which may be legislated upon and settled at this session:

First. That the States shall be required to afford the opportunity of a good common-school education to every child within their limits.

Second. No sectarian tenets shall ever be taught in any school supported in whole or in part by the State, nation, or by the proceeds of any tax levied upon any community. Make education compulsory so far as to deprive all persons who can not read and write from becoming voters after the year 1890, disfranchising none, however, on grounds of illiteracy who may be voters at the time this amendment takes effect.

Third. Declare church and state forever separate and distinct, but each free within their proper spheres; and that all church property shall bear its own proportion of taxation.

Fourth. Drive out licensed immorality, such as polygamy and the importation of women for illegitimate purposes. To recur again to the centennial year, it would seem as though now, as we are about to begin the second century of our national existence, would be a most fitting time for these reforms.

Fifth. Enact such laws as will insure a speedy return to a sound currency, such as will command the respect of the world.

Believing that these views will commend themselves to the great majority of the right-thinking and patriotic citizens of the United States, I submit the rest to Congress.

U. S. GRANT

December 5, 1876
To the Senate and House of Representatives:

In submitting my eighth and last annual message to Congress it seems proper that I should refer to and in some degree recapitulate the events and official acts of the past eight years.

It was my fortune, or misfortune, to be called to the office of Chief Executive without any previous political training. From the age of 17 I had never even witnessed the excitement attending a Presidential campaign but twice antecedent to my own candidacy, and at but one of them was I eligible as a voter.

Under such circumstances it is but reasonable to suppose that errors of judgment must have occurred. Even had they not, differences of opinion between the Executive, bound by an oath to the strict performance of his duties, and writers and debaters must have arisen. It is not necessarily evidence of blunder on the part of the Executive because there are these differences of views. Mistakes have been made, as all can see and I admit, but it seems to me oftener in the selections made of the assistants appointed to aid in carrying out the various duties of administering the Government—in nearly every case selected without a personal acquaintance with the appointee, but upon recommendations of the representatives chosen directly by the people. It is impossible, where so many trusts are to be allotted, that the right parties should be chosen in every instance. History shows that no Administration from the time of Washington to the present has been free from these mistakes. But I leave comparisons to history, claiming only that I have acted in every instance from a conscientious desire to do what was right, constitutional, within the law, and for the very best interests of the whole people. Failures have been errors of judgment, not of intent.

My civil career commenced, too, at a most critical and difficult time. Less than four years before, the country had emerged from a conflict such as no other nation had ever survived. Nearly one-half of the States had revolted against the Government, and of those remaining faithful to the Union a large percentage of the population sympathized with the rebellion and made an "enemy in the rear" almost as dangerous as the more honorable enemy in the front. The latter committed errors of judgment, but they maintained them openly and courageously; the former received the protection of the Government they would see destroyed, and reaped all the pecuniary advantage to be gained out of the then existing state of affairs, many of them by obtaining contracts and by swindling the Government in the delivery of their goods.

Immediately on the cessation of hostilities the then noble President, who had carried the country so far through its perils, fell a martyr to his patriotism at the hands of an assassin.

The intervening time to my first inauguration was filled up with wranglings between Congress and the new Executive as to the best mode of "reconstruction," or, to speak plainly, as to whether the control of the Government should be thrown immediately into the hands of those who had so recently and persistently tried to destroy it, or whether the victors should continue to have an equal voice with them in this control. Reconstruction, as finally agreed upon, means this and only this, except that the late slave was enfranchised, giving an increase, as was supposed, to the Union-loving and Union-supporting votes. If free in the full sense of the word, they would not disappoint this expectation. Hence at the beginning of my first Administration the work of reconstruction, much embarrassed by the long delay, virtually commenced. It was the work of the legislative branch of the Government. My province was wholly in approving their acts, which I did most heartily, urging the legislatures of States that had not yet done so to ratify the fifteenth amendment to the Constitution. The country was laboring under an enormous debt, contracted in the suppression of rebellion, and taxation was so oppressive as to discourage production. Another danger also threatened us—a foreign war. The last difficulty had to be adjusted and was adjusted without a war and in a manner highly honorable to all parties concerned. Taxes have been reduced within the last seven years nearly $300,000,000, and the national debt has been reduced in the same time over $435,000,000. By refunding the 6 per cent bonded debt for bonds bearing 5 and 4 1/2 per cent interest, respectively, the annual interest has been reduced from over $130,000,000 in 1869 to but little over $100,000,000 in 1876. The balance of trade has been changed from over $130,000,000 against the United States in 1869 to more than $120,000,000 in our favor in 1876.

It is confidently believed that the balance of trade in favor of the United States will increase, not diminish, and that the pledge of Congress to resume specie payments in 1879 will be easily accomplished, even in the absence of much-desired further legislation on the subject.

A policy has been adopted toward the Indian tribes inhabiting a large portion of the territory of the United States which has been humane and has substantially ended Indian hostilities in the whole land except in a portion of Nebraska, and Dakota, Wyoming, and Montana Territories—the Black Hills region and approaches thereto. Hostilities there have grown out of the avarice of the white man, who has violated our treaty stipulations in his search for gold. The question might be asked why the Government has not enforced obedience to the terms of the treaty prohibiting the occupation of the Black Hills region by whites. The answer is simple: The first immigrants to the Black Hills were removed by troops, but rumors of rich discoveries of gold took into that region increased numbers. Gold has actually been found in paying quantity, and an effort to remove the miners would only result in the desertion of the bulk of the troops that might be sent there to remove them. All difficulty in this matter has, however, been removed—subject to the approval of Congress—by a treaty ceding the Black Hills and approaches to settlement by citizens.

The subject of Indian policy and treatment is so fully set forth by the Secretary of the Interior and the Commissioner of Indian Affairs, and my views so fully expressed therein, that I refer to their reports and recommendations as my own.

The relations of the United States with foreign powers continue on a friendly footing.

Questions have arisen from time to time in the foreign relations of the Government, but the United States have been happily free during the past year from the complications and embarrassments which have surrounded some of the foreign powers.

The diplomatic correspondence submitted herewith contains information as to certain of the matters which have occupied the Government.

The cordiality which attends our relations with the powers of the earth has been plainly shown by the general participation of foreign nations in the exhibition which has just closed and by the exertions made by distant powers to show their interest in and friendly feelings toward the United States in the commemoration of the centennial of the nation. The Government and people of the United States have not only fully appreciated this exhibition of kindly feeling, but it may be justly and fairly expected that no small benefits will result both to ourselves and other nations from a better acquaintance, and a better appreciation of our mutual advantages and mutual wants.

Congress at its last session saw fit to reduce the amount usually appropriated for foreign intercourse by withholding appropriations for representatives of the United States in certain foreign countries and for certain consular officers, and by reducing the amounts usually appropriated for certain other diplomatic posts, and thus necessitating a change in the grade of the representatives. For these reasons, immediately upon the passage of the bill making appropriations for the diplomatic and consular service for the present fiscal year, instructions were issued to the representatives of the United States at Bolivia, Ecuador, and Colombia, and to the consular officers for whom no appropriation had been made, to close their respective legations and consulates and cease from the performance of their duties; and in like manner steps were immediately taken to substitute charge's d'affaires for ministers resident in Portugal, Denmark, Greece, Switzerland, and Paraguay.

While thoroughly impressed with the wisdom of sound economy in the foreign service, as in other branches of the Government, I can not escape the conclusion that in some instances the withholding of appropriations will prove an expensive economy, and that the small retrenchment secured by a change of grade in certain diplomatic posts is not an adequate consideration for the loss of influence and importance which will attend our foreign representatives under this reduction. I am of the opinion that a reexamination of the subject will cause a change in some instances in the conclusions reached on these subjects at the last session of Congress.

The Court of Commissioners of Alabama Claims, whose functions were continued by an act of the last session of Congress until the 1st day of January, 1877, has carried on its labors with diligence and general satisfaction. By a report from the clerk of the court, transmitted herewith, bearing date November 14, 1876, it appears that within the time now allowed by law the court will have disposed of all the claims presented for adjudication. This report also contains a statement of the general results of the labors of the court to the date thereof. It is a cause of satisfaction that the method adopted for the satisfaction of the classes of claims submitted to the court, which are of long standing and justly entitled to early consideration, should have proved successful and acceptable.

It is with satisfaction that I am enabled to state that the work of the joint commission for determining the boundary line between the United States and British possessions from the northwest angle of the Lake of the Woods to the Rocky Mountains, commenced in 1872, has been completed. The final agreements of the commissioners, with the maps, have been duly signed, and the work of the commission is complete.

The fixing of the boundary upon the Pacific coast by the protocol of March 10, 1873, pursuant to the award of the Emperor of Germany by Article XXXIV of the treaty of Washington, with the termination of the work of this commission, adjusts and fixes the entire boundary between the United States and the British possessions, except as to the portion of territory ceded by Russia to the United States under the treaty of 1867. The work intrusted to the commissioner and the officers of the Army attached to the commission has been well and satisfactorily performed. The original of the final agreement of the commissioners, signed upon the 29th of May, 1876, with the original official "lists of astronomical stations observed," the original official "list of monuments marking the international boundary line," and the maps, records, and general reports relating to the commission, have been deposited in the Department of State. The official report of the commissioner on the part of the United States, with the report of the chief astronomer of the United States, will be submitted to Congress within a short time.

I reserve for a separate communication to Congress a statement of the condition of the questions which lately arose with Great Britain respecting the surrender of fugitive criminals under the treaty of 1842.

The Ottoman Government gave notice, under date of January 15, 1874, of its desire to terminate the treaty of 1862, concerning commerce and navigation, pursuant to the provisions of the twenty-second article thereof. Under this notice the treaty terminated upon the 5th day of June, 1876. That Government has invited negotiations toward the conclusion of a new treaty.

By the act of Congress of March 23, 1874, the President was authorized, when he should receive satisfactory information that the Ottoman Government or that of Egypt had organized new tribunals likely to secure to citizens of the United States the same impartial justice enjoyed under the exercise of judicial functions by diplomatic and consular officers of the United States, to suspend the operation of the act of June 22, 1860, and to accept for citizens of the United States the jurisdiction of the new tribunals. Satisfactory information having been received of the organization of such new tribunals in Egypt, I caused a proclamation to be issued upon the 27th of March last, suspending the operation of the act of June 22, 1860, in Egypt, according to the provisions of the act. A copy of the proclamation accompanies this message. The United States has united with the other powers in the organization of these courts. It is hoped that the jurisdictional questions which have arisen may be readily adjusted, and that this advance in judicial reform may be hindered by no obstacles.

The necessary legislation to carry into effect the convention respecting commercial reciprocity concluded with the Hawaiian Islands in 1875 having been had, the proclamation to carry into effect the convention, as provided by the act approved August 15, 1876, was duly issued upon the 9th day of September last. A copy thereof accompanies this message.

The commotions which have been prevalent in Mexico for some time past, and which, unhappily, seem to be not yet wholly quieted, have led to complaints of citizens of the United States of injuries by persons in authority. It is hoped, however, that these will ultimately be adjusted to the satisfaction of both Governments. The frontier of the United States in that quarter has not been exempt from acts of violence by citizens of one Republic on those of the other. The frequency of these is supposed to be increased and their adjustment made more difficult by the considerable changes in the course of the lower part of the Rio Grande River, which river is a part of the boundary between the two countries. These changes have placed on either side of that river portions of land which by existing conventions belong to the jurisdiction of the Government on the opposite side of the river. The subject of adjustment of this cause of difficulty is under consideration between the two Republics.

The Government of the United States of Colombia has paid the award in the case of the steamer Montijo, seized by authorities of that Government some years since, and the amount has been transferred to the claimants.

It is with satisfaction that I am able to announce that the joint commission for the adjustment of claims between the United States and Mexico under the convention of 1868, the duration of which has been several times extended, has brought its labors to a close. From the report of the agent of the United States, which accompanies the papers transmitted herewith, it will be seen that within the time limited by the commission 1,017 claims on the part of citizens of the United States against Mexico were referred to the commission. Of these claims 831 were dismissed or disallowed, and in 186 cases awards were made in favor of the claimants against the Mexican Republic, amounting in the aggregate to $4,125,622.20. Within the same period 998 claims on the part of citizens of the Mexican Republic against the United States were referred to the commission. Of these claims 831 were dismissed or disallowed, and in 167 cases awards were made in favor of the claimants against the United States, amounting in the aggregate to $150,498.41.

By the terms of the convention the amount of these awards is to be deducted from the amount awarded in favor of our citizens against Mexico, and the balance only to be paid by Mexico to the United States, leaving the United States to make provision for this proportion of the awards in favor of its Own citizens.

I invite your attention to the legislation which will be necessary to provide for the payment.

In this connection I am pleased to be able to express the acknowledgments due to Sir Edward Thornton, the umpire of the commission, who has given to the consideration of the large number of claims submitted to him much time, unwearied patience, and that firmness and intelligence which are well known to belong to the accomplished representative of Great Britain, and which are likewise recognized by the representative in this country of the Republic of Mexico.

Monthly payments of a very small part of the amount due by the Government of Venezuela to citizens of the United States on account of claims of the latter against that Government continue to be made with reasonable punctuality. That Government has proposed to change the system which it has hitherto pursued in this respect by issuing bonds for part of the amount of the several claims. The proposition, however, could not, it is supposed, properly be accepted, at least without the consent of the holders of certificates of the indebtedness of Venezuela. These are so much dispersed that it would be difficult, if not impossible, to ascertain their disposition on the subject.

In former messages I have called the attention of Congress to the necessity of legislation with regard to fraudulent naturalization and to the subject of expatriation and the election of nationality.

The numbers of persons of foreign birth seeking a home in the United States, the ease and facility with which the honest emigrant may, after the lapse of a reasonable time, become possessed of all the privileges of citizenship of the United States, and the frequent occasions which induce such adopted citizens to return to the country of their birth render the subject of naturalization and the safeguards which experience has proved necessary for the protection of the honest naturalized citizen of paramount importance. The very simplicity in the requirements of law on this question affords opportunity for fraud, and the want of uniformity in the proceedings and records of the various courts and in the forms of the certificates of naturalization issued affords a constant source of difficulty.

I suggest no additional requirements to the acquisition of citizenship beyond those now existing, but I invite the earnest attention of Congress to the necessity and wisdom of some provisions regarding uniformity in the records and certificates, and providing against the frauds which frequently take place and for the vacating of a record of naturalization obtained in fraud.

These provisions are needed in aid and for the protection of the honest citizen of foreign birth, and for the want of which he is made to suffer not infrequently. The United States has insisted upon the right of expatriation, and has obtained, after a long struggle, an admission of the principle contended for by acquiescence therein on the part of many foreign powers and by the conclusion of treaties on that subject. It is, however, but justice to the government to which such naturalized citizens have formerly owed allegiance, as well as to the United States, that certain fixed and definite rules should be adopted governing such cases and providing how expatriation may be accomplished.

While emigrants in large numbers become citizens of the United States, it is also true that persons, both native born and naturalized, once citizens of the United States, either by formal acts or as the effect of a series of facts and circumstances, abandon their citizenship and cease to be entitled to the protection of the United States, but continue on convenient occasions to assert a claim to protection in the absence of provisions on these questions. And in this connection I again invite your attention to the necessity of legislation concerning the marriages of American citizens contracted abroad, and concerning the status of American women who may marry foreigners and of children born of American parents in a foreign country.

The delicate and complicated questions continually occurring with reference to naturalization, expatriation, and the status of such persons as I have above referred to induce me to earnestly direct your attention again to these subjects.

In like manner I repeat my recommendation that some means be provided for the hearing and determination of the just and subsisting claims of aliens upon the Government of the United States within a reasonable limitation, and of such as may hereafter arise. While by existing provisions of law the Court of Claims may in certain cases be resorted to by an alien claimant, the absence of any general provisions governing all such cases and the want of a tribunal skilled in the disposition of such cases upon recognized fixed and settled principles, either provides no remedy in many deserving cases or compels a consideration of such claims by Congress or the executive department of the Government.

It is believed that other governments are in advance of the United States upon this question, and that the practice now adopted is entirely unsatisfactory.

Congress, by an act approved the 3d day of March, 1875, authorized the inhabitants of the Territory of Colorado to form a State government, with the name of the State of Colorado, and therein provided for the admission of said State, when formed, into the Union upon an equal footing with the original States.

A constitution having been adopted and ratified by the people of that State, and the acting governor having certified to me the facts as provided by said act, together with a copy of such constitution and ordinances as provided for in the said act, and the provisions of the said act of Congress having been duly complied with, I issued a proclamation upon the 1st of August,

1876, a copy of which is hereto annexed.

The report of the Secretary of War shows that the Army has been actively employed during the year in subduing, at the request of the Indian Bureau, certain wild bands of the Sioux Indian Nation and in preserving the peace at the South during the election. The commission constituted under the act of July 24, 1876, to consider and report on the "whole subject of the reform and reorganization of the Army" met in August last, and has collected a large mass of statistics and opinions bearing on the subject before it. These are now under consideration, and their report is progressing. I am advised, though, by the president of the commission that it will be impracticable to comply with the clause of the act requiring the report to be presented, through me, to Congress on the first day of this session, as there has not yet been time for that mature deliberation which the importance of the subject demands. Therefore I ask that the time of making the report be extended to the 29th day of January, 1877.

In accordance with the resolution of August 15, 1876, the Army regulations prepared under the act of March 1, 1875, have not been promulgated, but are held until after the report of the above-mentioned commission shall have been received and acted on.

By the act of August 15, 1876, the cavalry force of the Army was increased by 2,500 men, with the proviso that they should be discharged on the expiration of hostilities. Under this authority the cavalry regiments have been strengthened, and a portion of them are now in the field pursuing the remnants of the Indians with whom they have been engaged during the summer.

The estimates of the War Department are made up on the basis of the number of men authorized by law, and their requirements as shown by years of experience, and also with the purpose on the part of the bureau officers to provide for all contingencies that may arise during the time for which the estimates are made. Exclusive of engineer estimates (presented in accordance with acts of Congress calling for surveys and estimates for improvements at various localities), the estimates now presented are about six millions in excess of the appropriations for the years 1874-75 and 1875-76. This increase is asked in order to provide for the increased cavalry force (should their services be necessary), to prosecute economically work upon important public buildings, to provide for armament of fortifications and manufacture of small arms, and to replenish the working stock in the supply departments. The appropriations for these last named have for the past few years been so limited that the accumulations in store will be entirely exhausted during the present year, and it will be necessary to at once begin to replenish them.

I invite your special attention to the following recommendations of the Secretary of War:

First. That the claims under the act of July 4, 1864, for supplies taken by the Army during the war be removed from the offices of the Quartermaster and Commissary Generals and transferred to the Southern Claims Commission. These claims are of precisely similar nature to those now before the Southern Claims Commission, and the War Department bureaus have not the clerical force for their examination nor proper machinery for investigating the loyalty of the claimants.

Second. That Congress sanction the scheme of an annuity fund for the benefit of the families of deceased officers, and that it also provide for the permanent organization of the Signal Service, both of which were recommended in my last annual message.

Third. That the manufacturing operations of the Ordnance Department be concentrated at three arsenals and an armory, and that the remaining arsenals be sold and the proceeds applied to this object by the Ordnance Department.

The appropriations for river and harbor improvements for the current year were $5,015,000. With my approval, the Secretary of War directed that of this amount $2,000,000 should be expended, and no new works should be begun and none prosecuted which were not of national importance. Subsequently this amount was increased to $2,237,600, and the works are now progressing on this basis.

The improvement of the South Pass of the Mississippi River, under James B. Eads and his associates, is progressing favorably. At the present time there is a channel of 20.3 feet in depth between the jetties at the mouth of the pass and 18.5 feet at the head of the pass. Neither channel, however, has the width required before payments can be made by the United States. A commission of engineer officers is now examining these works, and their reports will be presented as soon as received.

The report of the Secretary of the Navy shows that branch of the service to be in condition as effective as it is possible to keep it with the means and authority given the Department. It is, of course, not possible to rival the costly and progressive establishments of great European powers with the old material of our Navy, to which no increase has been authorized since the war, except the eight small cruisers built to supply the place of others which had gone to decay. Yet the most has been done that was possible with the means at command; and by substantially rebuilding some of our old ships with durable material and completely repairing and refitting our monitor fleet the Navy has been gradually so brought up that, though it does not maintain its relative position among the progressive navies of the world, it is now in a condition more powerful and effective than it ever has been in time of peace.

The complete repairs of our five heavy ironclads are only delayed on account of the inadequacy of the appropriations made last year for the working bureaus of the Department, which were actually less in amount than those made before the war, notwithstanding the greatly enhanced price of labor and materials and the increase in the cost of the naval service growing out of the universal use and great expense of steam machinery. The money necessary for these repairs should be provided at once, that they may be completed without further unnecessary delay and expense.

When this is done, all the strength that there is in our Navy will be developed and useful to its full capacity, and it will be powerful for purposes of defense, and also for offensive action, should the necessity for that arise within a reasonable distance from our shores.

The fact that our Navy is not more modern and powerful than it is has been made a cause of complaint against the Secretary of the Navy by persons who at the same time criticise and complain of his endeavors to bring the Navy that we have to its best and most efficient condition; but the good sense of the country will understand that it is really due to his practical action that we have at this time any effective naval force at command.

The report of the Postmaster-General shows the excess of expenditures (excluding expenditures on account of previous years) over receipts for the fiscal year ended June 30, 1876, to be $4,151,988.66.

Estimated expenditures for the fiscal year ending June 30, 1878, are $36,723,432.43.

Estimated revenue for same period is $30,645,165, leaving estimated excess of expenditure, to be appropriated as a deficiency, of $6,078,267.43.

The Postmaster-General, like his predecessor, is convinced that a change in the basis of adjusting the salaries of postmasters of the fourth class is necessary for the good of the service as well as for the interests of the Government, and urgently recommends that the compensation of the class of postmasters above mentioned be based upon the business of their respective offices, as ascertained from the sworn returns to the Auditor of stamps canceled.

A few postmasters in the Southern States have expressed great apprehension of their personal safety on account of their connection with the postal service, and have specially requested that their reports of apprehended danger should not be made public lest it should result in the loss of their lives. But no positive testimony of interference has been submitted, except in the case of a mail messenger at Spartanburg, in South Carolina, who reported that he had been violently driven away while in charge of the mails on account of his political affiliations. An assistant superintendent of the Railway Mail Service investigated this case and reported that the messenger had disappeared from his post, leaving his work to be performed by a substitute. The Postmaster-General thinks this case is sufficiently suggestive to justify him in recommending that a more severe punishment should be provided for the offense of assaulting any person in charge of the mails or of retarding or otherwise obstructing them by threats of personal injury.

"A very gratifying result is presented in the fact that the deficiency of this Department during the last fiscal year was reduced to $4,081,790.18, as against $6,169,938.88 of the preceding year. The difference can be traced to the large increase in its ordinary receipts (which greatly exceed the estimates therefor) and a slight decrease in its expenditures."

The ordinary receipts of the Post-Office Department for the past seven fiscal years have increased at an average of over 8 per cent per annum, while the increase of expenditures for the same period has been but about 5.50 per cent per annum, and the decrease of deficiency in the revenues has been at the rate of nearly 2 per cent per annum.

The report of the Commissioner of Agriculture accompanying this message will be found one of great interest, marking, as it does, the great progress of the last century in the variety of products of the soil; increased knowledge and skill in the labor of producing, saving, and manipulating the same to prepare them for the use of man; in the improvements in machinery to aid the agriculturist in his labors, and in a knowledge of those scientific subjects necessary to a thorough system of economy in agricultural production, namely, chemistry, botany, entomology, etc. A study of this report by those interested in agriculture and deriving their support from it will find it of value in pointing out those articles which are raised in greater quantity than the needs of the world require, and must sell, therefore, for less than the cost of production, and those which command a profit over cost of production because there is not an overproduction.

I call special attention to the need of the Department for a new gallery for the reception of the exhibits returned from the Centennial Exhibition, including the exhibits donated by very many foreign nations, and to the recommendations of the Commissioner of Agriculture generally.

The reports of the District Commissioners and the board of health are just received—too late to read them and to make recommendations thereon—and are herewith submitted.

The international exhibition held in Philadelphia this year, in commemoration of the one hundredth anniversary of American independence, has proven a great success, and will, no doubt, be of enduring advantage to the country. It has shown the great progress in the arts, sciences, and mechanical skill made in a single century, and demonstrated that we are but little behind older nations in any one branch, while in some we scarcely have a rival. It has served, too, not only to bring peoples and products of skill and labor from all parts of the world together, but in bringing together people from all sections of our own country, which must prove a great benefit in the information imparted and pride of country engendered.

It has been suggested by scientists interested in and connected with the Smithsonian Institution, in a communication herewith, that the Government exhibit be removed to the capital and a suitable building be erected or purchased for its accommodation as a permanent exhibit. I earnestly recommend this; and believing that Congress would second this view, I directed that all Government exhibits at the Centennial Exhibition should remain where they are, except such as might be injured by remaining in a building not intended as a protection in inclement weather, or such as may be wanted by the Department furnishing them, until the question of permanent exhibition is acted on.

Although the moneys appropriated by Congress to enable the participation of the several Executive Departments in the International Exhibition of 1876 were not sufficient to carry out the undertaking to the full extent at first contemplated, it gives me pleasure to refer to the very efficient and creditable manner in which the board appointed from these several Departments to provide an exhibition on the part of the Government have discharged their duties with the funds placed at their command. Without a precedent to guide them in the preparation of such a display, the success of their labors was amply attested by the sustained attention which the contents of the Government building attracted during the period of the exhibition from both foreign and native visitors.

I am strongly impressed with the value of the collection made by the Government for the purposes of the exhibition, illustrating, as it does, the mineral resources of the country, the statistical and practical evidences of our growth as a nation, and the uses of the mechanical arts and the applications of applied science in the administration of the affairs of Government.

Many nations have voluntarily contributed their exhibits to the United States to increase the interest in any permanent exhibition Congress may provide for. For this act of generosity they should receive the thanks of the people, and I respectfully suggest that a resolution of Congress to that effect be adopted.

The attention of Congress can not be too earnestly called to the necessity of throwing some greater safeguard over the method of choosing and declaring the election of a President. Under the present system there seems to be no provided remedy for contesting the election in any one State. The remedy is partially, no doubt, in the enlightenment of electors. The compulsory support of the free school and the disfranchisement of all who can not read and write the English language, after a fixed probation, would meet my hearty approval. I would not make this apply, however, to those already voters, but I would to all becoming so after the expiration of the probation fixed upon. Foreigners coming to this country to become citizens, who are educated in their own language, should acquire the requisite knowledge of ours during the necessary residence to obtain naturalization. If they did not take interest enough in our language to acquire sufficient knowledge of it to enable them to study the institutions and laws of the country intelligently, I would not confer upon them the right to make such laws nor to select those who do.

I append to this message, for convenient reference, a synopsis of administrative events and of all recommendations to Congress made by me during the last seven years. Time may show some of these recommendations not to have been wisely conceived, but I believe the larger part will do no discredit to the Administration. One of these recommendations met with the united opposition of one political party in the Senate and with a strong opposition from the other, namely, the treaty for the annexation of Santo Domingo to the United States, to which I will specially refer, maintaining, as I do, that if my views had been concurred in the country would be in a more prosperous condition to-day, both politically and financially.

Santo Domingo is fertile, and upon its soil may be grown just those tropical products of which the United States use so much, and which are produced or prepared for market now by slave labor almost exclusively, namely, sugar, coffee, dyewoods, mahogany, tropical fruits, tobacco, etc. About 75 per cent of the exports of Cuba are consumed in the United States. A large percentage of the exports of Brazil also find the same market. These are paid for almost exclusively in coin, legislation, particularly in Cuba, being unfavorable to a mutual exchange of the products of each country. Flour shipped from the Mississippi River to Havana can pass by the very entrance to the city on its way to a port in Spain, there pay a duty fixed upon articles to be reexported, transferred to a Spanish vessel and brought back almost to the point of starting, paying a second duty, and still leave a profit over what would be received by direct shipment. All that is produced in Cuba could be produced in Santo Domingo. Being a part of the United States, commerce between the island and mainland would be free. There would be no export duties on her shipments nor import duties on those coming here. There would be no import duties upon the supplies, machinery, etc., going from the States. The effect that would have been produced upon Cuban commerce, with these advantages to a rival, is observable at a glance. The Cuban question would have been settled long ago in favor of "free Cuba." Hundreds of American vessels would now be advantageously used in transporting the valuable woods and other products of the soil of the island to a market and in carrying supplies and emigrants to it. The island is but sparsely settled, while it has an area sufficient for the profitable employment of several millions of people. The soil would have soon fallen into the hands of United States capitalists. The products are so valuable in commerce that emigration there would have been encouraged; the emancipated race of the South would have found there a congenial home, where their civil rights would not be disputed and where their labor would be so much sought after that the poorest among them could have found the means to go. Thus in cases of great oppression and cruelty, such as has been practiced upon them in many places within the last eleven years, whole communities would have sought refuge in Santo Domingo. I do not suppose the whole race would have gone, nor is it desirable that they should go. Their labor is desirable—indispensable almost—where they now are. But the possession of this territory would have left the negro "master of the situation," by enabling him to demand his rights at home on pain of finding them elsewhere.

I do not present these views now as a recommendation for a renewal of the subject of annexation, but I do refer to it to vindicate my previous action in regard to it.

With the present term of Congress my official life terminates. It is not probable that public affairs will ever again receive attention from me further than as a citizen of the Republic, always taking a deep interest in the honor, integrity, and prosperity of the whole land.

U. S. GRANT